362.196
DO

At Issue

Do Infectious Diseases Pose a Threat?

Other Books in the At Issue Series:

At Issue

Do Infectious Diseases Pose a Threat?

Diane Andrews Henningfeld, Book Editor

GREENHAVEN PRESS
A part of Gale, Cengage Learning

GALE
CENGAGE Learning·

Detroit • New York • San Francisco • New Haven, Conn • Waterville, Maine • London

GALE
CENGAGE Learning·

Christine Nasso, *Publisher*
Elizabeth Des Chenes, *Managing Editor*

© 2009 Greenhaven Press, a part of Gale, Cengage Learning.

Gale and Greenhaven Press are registered trademarks used herein under license.

For more information, contact:
Greenhaven Press
27500 Drake Rd.
Farmington Hills, MI 48331-3535
Or you can visit our Internet site at gale.cengage.com

For product information and technology assistance, contact us at

Gale Customer Support, 1-800-877-4253
For permission to use material from this text or product, submit all requests online at www.cengage.com/permissions

Further permissions questions can be emailed to permissionrequest@cengage.com

Articles in Greenhaven Press anthologies are often edited for length to meet page requirements. In addition, original titles of these works are changed to clearly present the main thesis and to explicitly indicate the author's opinion. Every effort is made to ensure that Greenhaven Press accurately reflects the original intent of the authors. Every effort has been made to trace the owners of copyrighted material.

Cover photograph © Images.com/Corbis.

LIBRARY OF CONGRESS CATALOGING-IN-PUBLICATION DATA

Do infectious diseases pose a threat? / Diane Andrews Henningfeld, book editor.
    p. cm. -- (At issue)
Includes bibliographical references and index.
ISBN 978-0-7377-4294-7 (hardcover)
ISBN 978-0-7377-4293-0 (pbk.)
1. Communicable diseases--Popular works. 2. Emerging infectious diseases--Popular works. 3. Epidemics--Popular works. I. Henningfeld, Diane Andrews.
RA643.D595 2009
362.196'9--dc22

                                                    2008049414

Printed in the United States of America
2 3 4 5 6 7 13 12 11 10 09

Contents

Introduction

In 1917, the United States entered World War I, providing fresh troops and supplies to the war-weary English and French Allied forces. The Americans, however, unwittingly brought with them an unwanted guest in the spring of 1918, a deadly influenza virus that would span the globe and kill some 30 million to 50 million individuals before finally burning out.

While commonly called "Spanish influenza," researchers such as John Barry, in his book *The Great Influenza*, and Alfred Crosby, in his *America's Forgotten Pandemic*, place the first known cases of the H1N1 influenza strain in Haskell, Kansas, in the spring of 1918. At the time, doctors were not required to inform the Public Health Service of flu cases; thus, there is no clear picture of how widespread the first wave of influenza was. Haskell, however, is located very near Camp Funston, where large numbers of young men were gathering for training before being shipped out to the war. According to Crosby, "Beginning on March 4, 1918, masses of soldiers at Camp Funston, Kansas, poured into the camp hospital with fever, headache, backache, and, in general, with all the symptoms of grippe [a then-common name for influenza]." Within a short time, other camps reported many of their men to be sick as well. Likewise, other institutions such as prisons also reported a high rate of infection from a particularly virulent strain of flu. The death rate from the first wave of influenza in the spring of 1918 was not very high, however; most Americans who contracted the flu recovered quickly.

And that might have been the end of it, had not large numbers of young men, living in close quarters in army barracks and in even closer quarters on transport ships, carried the virus with them to Europe. By April 1918, both British and German troops were experiencing high rates of influenza, and by May, French troops were also affected. It is likely that the disease influenced the outcome of the war. According to Crosby, the German general Erich von Ludendorff "blamed the failure of his July offensive, which came so close to winning the war for Germany, on the poor morale and diminished strength of his armies, which he attributed in part to flu."

While the flu went quiet in the United States in the summer of 1918, it was busily infecting populations across the world, mutating as it worked its way through new hosts on new continents and becoming increasingly lethal. In June of 1918, for example, it is likely that British troops spread the disease to Russia. China, India, and many other countries also experienced widespread influenza infections. By the time the flu bug resurfaced in North America in September 1918, it had become a monster. People who contracted it were often dead within days, bleeding from their noses, their ears, and their mouths, their lungs totally destroyed. Most terrible of all, according to John Barry, was the fact that nearly half the people who died were young, healthy adults between the ages of twenty-five and thirty-five.

The epidemic in the United States spread rapidly, moving to Philadelphia where over twelve thousand people died in just four weeks. So many people died so quickly that the city had to build makeshift morgues. They ran out of coffins. There were not enough healthy people to care for the sick or dig graves for the dead. Public health offices were strained past their limits, and the very fabric of society was at risk of rupturing. Schools, businesses, and churches closed their doors, and public gatherings were outlawed. Telephone service ceased. Police, firefighters, and garbage collectors were unable to work. There were not enough nurses to provide even basic care for the ill. Young children were found at home without food or water, the adults in the household lying dead in bed.

Theses scenes were repeated across the United States, where an estimated 675,000 people died in just a few months, and millions were taken ill, according to David Morens and Anthony S. Fauci in an article appearing in the April 1, 2007, issue of the *Journal of Infectious Diseases*. This figure is greater than the total of all Americans who died in World War I, World War II, the Korean War, and the Vietnam War *combined*. About 5 percent of all those who contracted the flu in the United States died, and many more were permanently disabled.

Matters were complicated by war censorship; in order to avoid panic, reports of the flu epidemic were limited. In addition, many cities continued to hold war rallies to sell war bonds, leading to large gatherings of people. Further, human mobility, increased dramatically because of the war and new technologies, meant that the virus could easily travel around the world. Tim Appenzeller, in an October 2005 *National Geographic* article, quotes flu researcher Jeffrey Taubenberger: "Everybody on Earth breathed in the virus, and half of them got sick." In some Inuit communities of Alaska and Canada, not only did everyone get sick, everyone died. Scholars agree that the 1918 influenza pandemic killed more people in the shortest amount of time than any other epidemic in human history.

For years, the secrets of the 1918 influenza epidemic were buried with the dead. Researchers did not know why the flu had turned so deadly or why it attacked young people so brutally instead of the typical very young or elderly victims. In 2008, a few of these questions were answered. Highlighting research by Morens, Fauci, and Taubenberger, the *NIH News* issue of August 19, 2008, reported that Taubenberger discovered that "the predominant disease at the time of death appeared to have been bacterial pneumonia." Taubenberger also noted that "there was also evidence that the virus destroyed the cells lining the bronchial tubes. . . . This loss made other kinds of cells throughout the entire respiratory tract—including cells deep in the lungs—vulnerable to attack by bacteria that migrated down the newly created pathway from the nose to the throat."

The story of the influenza pandemic of 1918 is both fascinating and gruesome, a story that reveals the interplay of medicine, research, politics, and conflict in the modern world, and one that demonstrates the tremendous power of infectious disease to undermine modern advances in medical treatment. In the minds of many, the 1918 flu epidemic also seemed to be now firmly in the past. With the discovery of antibiotics and the development of effective vaccines, doctors, public officials, and the general population in the United States were confident that modern science had put an end to the threat of infectious diseases such as pandemic flu, polio, tuberculosis, and smallpox, among others, by the end of the twentieth century. However, the emergence of diseases such as SARS (severe acute respiratory syndrome) in 2002–2003, with its case-fatality rate of 9.6 percent, as reported by the World Health Organization in April 2003, shook the confidence of public health officials and the general public alike. In addition, the emergence of antibiotic-resistant strains of tuberculosis and the spread of avian influenza throughout Asia have raised worrisome issues. In fact, many scientists fear that it is only a matter of time before a strain of avian influenza will mutate to allow human-to-human transmission, an event that will usher in a deadly pandemic.

Thus, what appeared to be a final victory over infectious diseases in the middle of the twentieth century is proving to be merely a lull in the battle. The threat of infectious diseases still looms heavily over the world's population. The authors of *At Issue: Do Infectious Diseases Pose a Threat?* explore causes, methods of transmission, and ways to mitigate the risks. Climate change, political decisions, large-scale migrations, technological developments, the global economy: all will play a role as the world confronts old scourges and newly emerging diseases.

1

The Threat of Infectious Diseases: An Overview

Anthony S. Fauci, Nancy A. Touchette, and Gregory K. Folkers

Anthony S. Fauci is the director of the National Institute of Allergy and Infectious Diseases (NIAID), a division of the National Institutes of Health. Nancy A. Touchette is a special assistant to the director of the NIAID, and Gregory K. Folkers is the NIAID director's chief of staff.

Infectious disease has been a threat to humankind throughout history. In recent years diseases such as HIV/AIDS, West Nile fever, and severe acute respiratory syndrome (SARS) have joined malaria, tuberculosis, and influenza as causes for concern. Some of these have grown more dangerous as they have developed drug-resistant strains. Infectious diseases used as bioterrorism pose an additional threat to humans. Organizations such as the National Institute of Allergy and Infectious Diseases are leading the fight to prevent and combat such diseases through the development of vaccines and genetic research.

Infectious diseases have been an ever-present threat to mankind. From the biblical plagues and the Plague of Athens in ancient times, to the Black Death of the Middle Ages, the 1918 "Spanish Flu" pandemic, and more recently, the HIV/ AIDS pandemic, infectious diseases have continued to emerge and reemerge in a manner that defies accurate predictions.

Anthony S. Fauci, Nancy A. Touchette, and Gregory K. Folkers, "Emerging Infectious Diseases: A 10-Year Perspective from the National Institute of Allergy and Infectious Diseases," *Emerging Infectious Diseases*, vol. 11, April 2005, pp. 519–25. Reproduced by permission.

The past 10 years (1994–2004) have been no exception, as many new and reemerging microbial threats have continued to challenge the public health and infectious disease research communities worldwide. Since 1994, . . . significant strides in the global fight against the HIV/AIDS pandemic have been made. The infectious disease community has confronted several other newly emerging pathogens, such as the severe acute respiratory syndrome–associated coronavirus (SARS-CoV), henipaviruses (Hendra and Nipah), and, most recently, avian influenza viruses that have caused illness and deaths in humans with the threat of evolution into a pandemic. In addition, historically established infectious diseases, such as West Nile fever, human monkeypox, dengue, tuberculosis, and malaria have reemerged or resurged, sometimes in populations that previously had been relatively exempt from such affronts. Over the past decade, strains of common microbes such as *Staphylococcus aureus* and *Mycobacterium tuberculosis* have continued to develop resistance to the drugs that once were effective against them. Such antimicrobial-resistant microorganisms, which defy conventional therapies and pose a threat to public health, underscore the need for a robust pipeline of new antimicrobial agents based on innovative therapeutic strategies, new vaccines, and other preventive measures.

Although annual deaths . . . from infectious diseases have decreased over the past decade, the worldwide impact from infectious diseases remains substantial.

Perhaps most disturbing, the United States has recently [in 2001–2002] experienced a deliberately spread infectious disease in the form of 22 anthrax infections, including 5 anthrax-related deaths resulting from bioterrorism in 2001. These cases were accompanied by widespread psychological sequelae [aftereffects] and societal and economic disruptions.

Infectious Diseases Kill and Disable

These emerging and reemerging infectious diseases are super-imposed on a substantial baseline of established infectious diseases. Although annual deaths and lost years of healthy life from infectious diseases have decreased over the past decade, the worldwide impact from infectious diseases remains substantial. Overall, infectious diseases remain the third leading cause of death in the United States each year and the second leading cause of death worldwide. . . . Of the estimated 57 million deaths that occur throughout the world each year, [about] 15 million, [more than] 25%, are directly caused by infectious diseases. Millions more deaths are due to secondary effects of infections.

Infectious diseases also lead to compromised health and disability, accounting for nearly 30% of all disability-adjusted life years (DALYs) worldwide (1 disability-adjusted life year is 1 lost year of healthy life). Infectious diseases . . . contribute to the nearly 1.5 billion total DALYs each year. . . .

In the United States, the Centers for Disease Control and Prevention has devised strategies to prevent, monitor, and contain disease outbreaks. Within the National Institutes of Health [NIH], the National Institute of Allergy and Infectious Diseases (NIAID) is the lead agency for infectious disease research. . . .

The Threat of HIV/AIDS

HIV/AIDS has resulted in the death of [more than] 20 million persons throughout the world and is the leading cause of death among persons 15–59 years of age. Approximately 40 million persons are estimated to be living with HIV infection. In the United States, an estimated 1 million persons are infected with HIV, and 40,000 new infections occur each year. Since its recognition in 1981, the disease has killed more than half a million people in the United States.

Despite these grim statistics, reason for hope exists. Basic research has yielded major insights into the pathogenic mechanisms of HIV disease. This knowledge paved the way for the development of [more than] 20 antiretroviral medications approved by the Food and Drug Administration (FDA) that target HIV, as well as novel strategies for prevention and vaccine development.

With the use of combinations of drugs that target different proteins involved in HIV pathogenesis (a treatment strategy known as highly active antiretroviral therapy [HAART]), rates of death and illness in the United States and other industrialized countries have been dramatically reduced. Although the death rate due to HIV/AIDS in Europe and North America has fallen by 80% since HAART was introduced, relatively few people in poor countries have reaped these benefits. New initiatives such as the Global Fund to Fight AIDS, Tuberculosis, and Malaria and the President's Emergency Plan for AIDS Relief promise to greatly reduce the disparity between rich and poor countries with regard to access to HIV treatment, care, and prevention services.

The greatest challenge in HIV/AIDS research remains developing a vaccine that can either prevent the transmission of the virus or, failing that, halt progression to AIDS. . . .

The social, economic, and human toll exacted by malaria globally is widespread and profound.

Malaria Is Deadly

The social, economic, and human toll exacted by malaria globally is widespread and profound. Each year, acute malaria occurs in [more than] 300 million people and results in [more than] 1 million deaths worldwide. Most of these deaths occur in young children who live in sub-Saharan Africa.

In humans, the disease is caused by one of 4 species of *Plasmodium*, a single-cell parasite transmitted by anopheline

15

mosquitoes. In 2002, the complete genomic sequence of *Plasmodium falciparum* as well as that of the mosquito vector *Anopheles gambiae* were completed as the result of a multinational effort. With the genomic sequences of the parasite and its human and mosquito hosts now available, researchers have powerful tools to further characterize the genes and proteins involved in the life cycle of the parasite, and they are using this information to design effective drugs and vaccines.

Drug-resistant *Plasmodium* strains are widespread, as are insecticide-resistant strains of the mosquitoes that carry the parasites. Mutations in both parasites and mosquitoes that confer drug and insecticide resistance have been identified. For example, genetic analysis and molecular epidemiology studies of *P. falciparum* have shown that resistance to chloroquine and other antimalarials is caused by a mutation in a single gene.... This information is being used to track the spread of drug-resistant strains of the parasite and identify new drug targets. Researchers also are exploiting the new genomic information to create genetically altered mosquitoes that resist parasite infection and to develop new compounds that overcome or avoid resistance to existing pesticides.

Although influenza is commonplace and generally self-limited, an estimated 36,000 Americans die each year from complications of the disease.

Developing an effective antimalarial vaccine has been a challenge; however, an international research team recently developed a vaccine that shows promise in preventing malaria among children in Mozambique. The vaccine prevented infection and severe disease in a substantial percentage of children tested, a breakthrough with the potential of saving millions of lives....

Drug-Resistant TB on the Rise

Another ancient microbial scourge that has reemerged in recent years is tuberculosis (TB), caused by infection with the bacterium *Mycobacterium tuberculosis*. This infection is estimated to be prevalent in one third of the world's population. From this reservoir, 8 million new cases of TB develop worldwide each year that carry a death toll of [more than] 2 million. TB is especially prevalent among persons infected with HIV. The only currently available TB vaccine, . . . offers some protection, but its effect diminishes with time. TB drug treatment is effective, but adherence to lengthy therapeutic regimens is difficult to maintain, and multidrug-resistant TB is on the rise in many countries.

Researchers are applying state-of-the-art genomic and postgenomic techniques to identify key molecular pathways that could be exploited to develop improved TB interventions and vaccines. In 2004, for the first time in 60 years, 2 new vaccines designed to prevent TB entered phase 1 clinical trials in the United States. Many promising new anti-TB drug candidates also are now entering the drug pipeline. . . .

Influenza Can Kill

Each year, influenza develops in up to 20% of all Americans, and [more than] 200,000 are hospitalized with the disease. Although influenza is commonplace and generally self-limited, an estimated 36,000 Americans die each year from complications of the disease. Worldwide, severe influenza infections develop in 3–5 million people annually, and 250,000–500,000 deaths occur.

Outbreaks of avian influenza recently have drawn attention worldwide, particularly in Southeast Asia, where [as of April 2005] at least 55 persons have been infected and 42 have died since January 2004. The current strain of H5N1 avian influenza is highly pathogenic; it has killed millions of chickens and other birds. Although the virus can cross species to infect

17

humans, few suspected cases of human-to-human transmission have been reported. However, the virus could acquire characteristics that allow it to be readily transmitted among humans, which could cause a worldwide influenza pandemic, with the potential for killing millions of people. In 1918, a pandemic of the "Spanish Flu" killed 20–50 million people worldwide.

Recently, the NIH Influenza Genomics Project was initiated; it will conduct rapid sequencing of the complete genomes of the several thousand known avian and human influenza viruses as well as those that emerge in the future. Approximately 60 genomes are expected to be sequenced each month. This project should also illuminate the molecular basis of how new strains of influenza virus emerge and provide information on characteristics that contribute to increased virulence. Many researchers believe that the H5N1 virus shows the greatest potential for evolving into the next human pandemic strain. Avian H9N2 viruses also have infected humans and have the potential to cause a pandemic. To prepare for this possibility, the development of vaccines to prevent infection with H5N1 and H9N2 viral strains is being supported. . . .

Newly Emergent Diseases Spreading

West Nile virus (WNV), long endemic in Africa, West Asia, Europe, and the Middle East, represents a reemerging disease that only recently arrived in the United States. The virus first appeared in the New York City area in 1999, where WNV-related disease was reported in 62 persons. It has continued to spread throughout the United States in subsequent summers, infecting ever larger populations, particularly in 2003. Research has led to several promising vaccine candidates against WNV. One of these, based on a licensed yellow fever vaccine virus that contains 2 WNV genes, has been tested in nonhuman primates; it is currently being evaluated in human clinical trials. A second vaccine developed at NIH uses an attenuated dengue virus into which WNV genes have been inserted. This vaccine protects monkeys and horses against WNV infection, and a clinical trial is now underway. Subunit and DNA vaccines against WNV are also in various stages of development and testing. . . .

The emergence of SARS in Asia in late 2002, and the speed with which it was characterized and contained, underscores the importance of cooperation between researchers and public health officials. NIAID is focusing its resources on developing diagnostics, vaccines, and novel antiviral compounds to combat SARS-CoV. Basic research on the pathogenesis of the disease to identify appropriate targets for therapeutics and vaccines, as well as clinical studies to test new therapies, is also being supported. Among many projects that have received support are the development of a "SARS chip," a DNA microarray to rapidly identify SARS sequence variants, and a SARS diagnostic test based on polymerase chain reaction technology.

Researchers have developed 2 candidate vaccines, based on the SARS-CoV spike protein, that protect mice against SARS. Another promising vaccine protects against infection in monkeys when delivered intranasally [through the nose].

Infectious Diseases and Bioterrorism

The September 11, 2001, attacks on the World Trade Center and Pentagon, and the subsequent anthrax attacks that infected 22 people and killed 5, propelled the U.S. government to expand its biodefense research program. These studies are based on 3 approaches: basic research aimed at understanding structure, biology, and mechanisms by which potential bioweapons cause disease; studies to elucidate how the human immune system responds to these dangerous pathogens; and development of the technology to translate these basic studies into safe and effective countermeasures to detect, prevent, and treat diseases caused by such pathogens. . . .

The genomes of all biological agents considered to pose the most severe threats have been sequenced by researchers. In addition, programs have been expanded and contracts awarded to screen new chemical compounds as possible treatments for bioterror attacks. New animal models have been developed to test promising drugs, and repositories have been established to catalog reagents and specimens.

In addition, research to understand the body's protective mechanisms against pathogens is being pursued. The Cooperative Centers for Translational Research on Human Immunology and Biodefense will focus on studies of the human immune response to potential agents of bioterror, while other programs are focused on the innate immune system and the development of ways to boost innate immunity.

NIAID also has been very active in vaccine development as a biodefense countermeasure. The Institute has supported the development of a next-generation anthrax vaccine, known as recombinant protective antigen (rPA); it is undergoing clinical trials, and contracts for the Strategic National Stockpile to acquire it have recently been awarded. Several new smallpox vaccines also are being tested for safety and efficacy. . . .

If history is our guide, we can assume that the battle between the intellect and will of the human species and the extraordinary adaptability of microbes will be never-ending.

Challenges for the Future

Scientists—government and academic, together with their industrial partners and international collaborators—have made great strides over the past 10 years in understanding many of the pathogenic mechanisms of emerging and reemerging infectious diseases. Many of these discoveries have been translated into novel diagnostics, antiviral and antimicrobial compounds, and vaccines, often with extraordinary speed.

However many challenges remain. Paramount among these is developing a safe and effective HIV vaccine. The evolution of pathogens with resistance to antibacterial and antiviral agents continues to challenge us to better understand the mechanisms of drug resistance and to devise new ways to circumvent the problem. These efforts will pave the way for developing countermeasures against deliberately engineered microbes.

If history is our guide, we can assume that the battle between the intellect and will of the human species and the extraordinary adaptability of microbes will be never-ending. To successfully fight our microbial foes, we must continue to vigorously pursue research on the basic mechanisms that underlie microbial pathogenesis and develop novel strategies to outwit theses ingenious opponents. The past 10 years have been challenging but no more so than will be the future.

2

The World Is at Risk for an Influenza Pandemic

Roche Laboratories

Roche Laboratories is a research division of Hoffman-La Roche, Incorporated, a large multinational health-care and pharmaceutical company.

Influenza has caused large-scale epidemics, called pandemics, in the past, killing many millions of people. Because the influenza virus mutates quickly and frequently, humans cannot develop immunity to the disease. A large-scale pandemic such as the one that swept the world in 1918 could cause widespread social and economic disruption. Preparations for such an event include developing new vaccines and a plan for administering them. At present, the world is prepared to deal with neither a large influenza epidemic nor the havoc such an event would cause.

The word *pandemic* is used to describe a disease that affects people on a worldwide scale. Flu pandemics have occurred roughly every 20 to 30 years throughout history, the most serious being the misnamed "Spanish flu" of 1918, the "Asian flu" of 1957 and the "Hong Kong flu" of 1968.

Three conditions must be met to result in a pandemic:

1. The emergence of a new flu strain
2. The ability of that strain to infect humans and cause serious illness
3. The ability to spread easily among humans

Roche Laboratories, "Flu Pandemic Background," *Pandemic Planning Toolkit,* June 2006. Reproduced by permission.

Flu Pandemic Inevitable

Most experts agree that the question is not *if* another flu pandemic will occur, but *when*. But while some scientists worry that the current situation indicates a looming pandemic, others doubt that there is any immediate danger. Regardless of whether a pandemic occurs in the next year or the next 50 years, however, the consensus among public health officials is that we should prepare ourselves for this eventuality now. . . .

A flu pandemic occurs when a new flu virus appears against which the human population has no immunity. This results in several simultaneous epidemics worldwide, with enormous numbers of infections and deaths. With the increase in global transport and communications, as well as urbanization and overcrowded conditions, epidemics due to the new flu virus are likely to take hold quickly around the world.

Pandemic flu doesn't discriminate. In the worst pandemic of all time, the "Spanish flu" of 1918, as many as 50 million people perished worldwide. This pandemic caused most deaths in young and healthy persons in the age range of 15 to 35 years. In a complete reversal of previous patterns, 99% of deaths occurred in people younger than 65 years. The "milder" flu pandemic that occurred during 1968 and 1969 killed 1 million people across the globe.

The evolution of flu viruses cannot be predicted. This makes it difficult to know if or when a virus might mutate to become easily transmittable among humans. Therefore, it is impossible to say when another pandemic will arise, or whether it will be mild or severe.

An especially severe pandemic could lead to widespread illness, a large number of deaths and economic loss.

However, the World Health Organization [WHO] asserts that once a virus allows for efficient human-to-human transmission, a pandemic can occur. Because of high global mobility and interconnection, illness could spread quickly, and, if the virus has a high fatality rate, threaten millions of lives around the world.

Pandemics are a reality. Health records show at least 10 influenza pandemics over the past 300 years. . . .

The Impact of a Flu Pandemic

A flu pandemic may strike in waves, each of which could last for 6 to 8 weeks. An especially severe pandemic could lead to widespread illness, a large number of deaths and economic loss. Everyday life would be disrupted because so many people in so many places would become seriously ill at the same time. Impact could range from school and business closings to the interruption of such basic services as public transportation and food delivery.

A substantial portion of the world's population would require some form of medical care. Healthcare facilities would be overwhelmed, creating a strain on hospital staff and a shortage of beds, ventilators and other supplies. To cope with the demand, "surge capacity" at nontraditional sites, such as schools, may need to be created. The need for vaccine is likely to outstrip supply, and the supply of antiviral drugs is also likely to be inadequate early in a pandemic. Difficult decisions would need to be made regarding who gets the vaccinations and antiviral therapy. . . .

Central to preparedness planning is estimating the mortality rate of the next pandemic. Experts' answers to this fundamental question have ranged from 2 million to more than 50 million. All of these predictions are scientifically grounded. The reasons for the wide range of estimates are numerous.

Some estimates are based on extrapolations from past pandemics but significant details of these events are disputed, such as the true numbers of resulting deaths. The most precise predictions are based on the pandemic in 1968, but even in this case, estimates vary from 1 million to 4 million deaths.

Similarly, the number of deaths from the "Spanish flu" pandemic of 1918 is posited by different investigators to range from 20 million to well over 50 million.

Extrapolations are problematic because the world of today is a different place from the world of 1918. The impact of greatly improved nutrition and healthcare needs to be weighed against the contribution that the increase in international travel would have on global spread. The specific characteristics of a future pandemic virus cannot be predicted. It may affect 20% to 50% of the total population. It is also unknown how pathogenic a novel virus would be. . . .

Even in the best-case scenarios of the next pandemic, 2 to 7 million people could die and tens of millions could require medical attention worldwide. . . .

Effective Interventions

Researchers from the Los Alamos National Laboratory [in New Mexico] evaluated the effectiveness of different intervention strategies for a flu pandemic by developing a model that represents the US population and tests different properties of a potential pandemic flu virus. They found that, depending on the contagiousness of the virus, a variety of approaches could reduce the number of flu cases to fewer than that of an annual flu season.

The scientists simulated a virtual outbreak on computers at the Los Alamos National Laboratory. The researchers tested different interventions: distributing antiviral treatments to infected individuals and others near them to reduce symptoms and susceptibility; vaccinating people, possibly children first, with either 1 or 2 shots of a vaccine not well matched to the strain that may emerge; social distancing, such as restricting travel and quarantining households; and closing schools.

The results showed that, with *no* intervention, a pandemic flu with low contagiousness could peak after 117 days and infect about 33% of the US population. A highly contagious virus could peak after 64 days and infect about 54% of the population.

The researchers then compared what might happen in scenarios involving the use of different interventions. When the simulated virus was less contagious, the 3 most effective single measures included: distributing several million courses of antiviral treatment to targeted groups 7 days after a pandemic alert; school closures; and vaccinating 10 million people per week with 1 dose of a poorly matched vaccine. The results also showed that vaccinating school children first is more effective than random vaccination when the vaccine supply is limited. Regardless of contagiousness, social distancing measures, alone, had little effect. But when the virus was highly contagious, all single-intervention strategies left nearly half the population infected. In this instance, the only measures that reduced the number of cases to below the annual flu rate involved a combination of at least three different interventions, including a minimum of 182 million courses of antiviral treatment.

Economic Impact of a Pandemic

A pandemic could deliver a "shock" to the economy, with immediate demand- and supply-side effects, as well as longer-term supply-side effects.

The general slowdown in economic activity would reduce gross domestic product (GDP). Business confidence would be dented, the supply of labor would be restricted, supply chains would be strained as transportation systems were disrupted and arrears [late] and default rates on consumer and business debt would probably rise. It seems likely that the stock market would initially fall and rebound later.

Estimates of the economic impact vary widely. A pandemic could cause a serious recession in the US economy, with immediate costs ranging from $500 billion to $675 billion. The following is a sampling of predictions from financial leaders:

- *WBB Securities LLC* predicted that a pandemic could cause a 1-year economic loss of $488 billion and a permanent economic loss of $1.4 trillion to the US economy

- *The Congressional Budget Office* said a pandemic could deal a $675 billion hit to the US economy

- *The World Bank* has predicted that a pandemic could cost the global economy $800 billion a year

Despite the advance warning, the world is ill-prepared to defend itself against a flu pandemic.

Social and Educational Impact

In all likelihood, during the spread of a flu pandemic, international travel would dramatically decline as people avoided flu "hotspots" and governments restricted travel. People would quarantine themselves and their families by staying at home more. Nonessential activities requiring social contact would be sharply curtailed, leading to significant declines in retail trade. People would avoid public places, such as shopping malls, community centers, places of worship and public transit. Attendance at theaters, sporting events, museums and restaurants would decline.

It seems likely that many schools would close, and even if they did not, attendance would fall dramatically as parents kept their children at home. In either event, large-scale school closings would lead to a spike in workplace absences because parents would stay home to care for their children even if they were not sick. The impact on businesses of all kinds due to employee absenteeism would be dramatic. Many would close, at least temporarily. . . .

World Not Prepared

Despite the advance warning, the world is ill-prepared to defend itself against a flu pandemic. WHO has urged all countries to develop preparedness plans, but only approximately 40 have done so. WHO has further urged countries with adequate resources to stockpile antiviral drugs nationally for use at the start of a pandemic. Under the current situation, most developing countries may have limited access to vaccines and antiviral drugs throughout the duration of a pandemic.

3

The United States Is Prepared for an Influenza Pandemic

Michael O. Leavitt

Michael O. Leavitt is the former secretary of the U.S. Department of Health and Human Services.

The United States government is preparing for the next influenza pandemic by stockpiling vaccines, boosting vaccine production, and supporting research into new vaccines. In addition, the government is using new communication tools such as blogs and the Internet as well as traditional information-gathering techniques to encourage widespread participation in planning. Finally, the government has launched a public information campaign to help local leaders prepare for a pandemic. Thorough preparation will lessen the impact of any potential pandemic.

Forty million people died when the last major influenza pandemic swept around the world in 1918. We have seen two less severe pandemics since then. We will no doubt see another sometime in the future. We don't know when, and we don't know how bad it will be. But we know it will happen sooner or later and that what we do now will save lives—maybe millions of lives—in the future.

We have come a long way since November 2005, when President [George W.] Bush mobilized the nation to prepare for an influenza pandemic. HHS [U.S. Department of Health and Human Services] continues to play a prominent role in

Michael O. Leavitt, "Message from the Secretary," *Pandemic Planning Update V*, U.S. Department of Health and Human Services, March 17, 2008. U.S. Department of Health and Human Services.

pandemic preparedness, giving highest priority to those tasks that it is best positioned or uniquely able to undertake. These include:

- stockpiling pre-pandemic vaccine and antiviral drugs;

- providing financial and technical assistance to States to help them, among other things, create complementary stockpiles of antiviral drugs and develop and test various mitigation strategies;

- creating a domestic vaccine production capacity commensurate with the expected requirements of a pandemic;

- sponsoring advanced development projects toward the next generation of vaccines, therapeutics, and diagnostics. . . .

[We have already passed] many . . . important milestones. . . . We have licensed the first H5N1 influenza vaccine for humans and stockpiled enough antiviral medicine to treat 40 million Americans. We have committed over $1 billion to diversify influenza vaccine production technology. And we have worked with the world's leading vaccine companies to accelerate the development of cell-based influenza vaccine production to increase the nation's domestic vaccine production capacity. We have also invested heavily in clinical research and surveillance programs here at home and around the world.

We have held flu summits in every State of the Union, plus our first on-line "blog summit" [in] June [2007]. We have organized, equipped, and trained response teams and begun to modernize the U.S. Public Health Service Commissioned Corps to enhance its response capabilities. . . .

Collaboration Is Necessary

We have entered a new phase in our preparations. The milestones are farther apart but no less significant. We are now tackling some challenging issues that can only be resolved with the collaboration of the full range of stakeholders—State and local officials, public health and medical professionals, religious leaders and ethicists, the business community, organized labor, non-governmental organizations, and individuals from all walks of life. Each is needed to find the best answers to difficult questions such as "How do we decide who receives the first vaccines from our limited supplies?" and "Who should be responsible for stockpiling medical countermeasures such as facemasks, respirators, ventilators, and antiviral medications?"

These issues will have a significant impact on how States, counties, cities, communities, corporations, families, and individuals prepare for and respond to pandemic disease. None can be addressed fairly and fully without the participation of the persons likely to be affected.

We have mounted an unprecedented effort on the part of the Department and the Federal government to garner thoughts and comments on these issues from as many people as possible, using new communication tools such as blogs and web casts as well as large public forums, smaller group meetings, and conference calls.

A Vaccine Allocation Plan

In December 2007, the Department held its first ever web dialogue to discuss the proposed vaccine allocation plan. More than 400 people from 37 States took part in the five-day online conversation with Federal, State, and local health officials. The web dialogue followed two public meetings on vaccine allocation, in Henderson, NC, and Milwaukee, WI. We have also met with various stakeholder representatives to discuss the feedback from the public meetings and the web dialogue.

A cross-government working group was then tasked with defining a priority order for administering vaccine to counter an influenza pandemic. That group now is weighing the information received from the rounds of public consultation and is updating an earlier draft document to accommodate the most persuasive comments and critiques. The intent is to have a plan suitable for public release [by 2008]. . . .

Preparedness [for an influenza pandemic] is a process— learning, adapting, and growing.

Through the fall of 2007, we also held nearly twenty meetings around the country to discuss the shared responsibility concept of stockpiling medical countermeasures and the feasibility of private-sector stockpiling of antivirals. These meetings included senior leaders and subject matter specialists from throughout the Federal government, along with governors, mayors, State and local health officials, employers, health care providers, first responders, organized labor and law enforcement. Some meetings were conducted by conference call, but we also met in Atlanta, GA, Seattle, WA, Scottsdale, AZ, the Raleigh-Durham, NC, area, and Washington, DC.

Pandemic Planning

In December [2007], we launched a public education campaign to encourage people to prepare now for a future pandemic. The campaign, titled *Take the Lead: Working Together to Prepare Now*, is aimed at community leaders such as clergy, employers, and health care providers, and is designed to provide them with the information they need to communicate the importance of pandemic planning by families and individuals. It was developed after consultation with over a hundred leading organizations such as the American Medical Association, Catholic Health Association, Red Cross, Lions Clubs, and the U.S. Chamber of Commerce. We also held our first-ever blog featuring ten prominent leaders blogging over a five-week period on the subject of individual pandemic planning. The blog attracted more than 35,000 individual visitors, 1,600 comments, and more than 300 in-bound links from other websites, blogs and message boards.

There's still much to be done. Preparedness is a process—learning, adapting, and growing. We will continue these unprecedented efforts to reach out to stakeholders for help in shaping some of the most difficult pandemic planning issues. We will also be finalizing policies and guidance based on the input we have received thus far.

It is every American's continued commitment that will make our country a safer and a healthier place.

The Next Flu Pandemic

The media buzz has died down, but the "bird flu" virus has not. Avian influenza is still highly pathogenic, inflicting a heavy toll on domestic and wild bird populations in Asia, Europe, and Africa and, from time to time, infecting humans. To date, some 370 people have contracted the disease, largely through exposure to sick or dead birds; 235 of them have died.

We don't know if the H5N1 virus will spark the next pandemic, but we know that it's just a matter of time before something does. There is simply no reason to believe that this century will be different than any past century. The difference now is that we better understand the threat, so we can increase our preparedness for a pandemic before it comes, in order to diminish its potential impact.

The Federal government cannot mount an effective response to the threats that we face as a nation without partners at every level of government and throughout society. It is every American's continued commitment that will make our country a safer and a healthier place.

4

Avian Influenza Is a Threat to College Campuses

Susan Gurevitz

Susan Gurevitz is a public relations and marketing professional with a background in journalism. She writes about finances, insurance, and human resources in a business setting.

Because the 1918 influenza pandemic targeted otherwise healthy college-aged young adults, universities and colleges are worried about the risks such a pandemic would pose today. College campuses are particularly vulnerable to influenza because students live and eat in close quarters; visitors from other campuses, including athletic teams, often intermingle with students; and students engage in international travel. These factors make it easier for the disease to be transmitted. Risk management firms are helping colleges prepare themselves for many different contingencies. Being prepared before a pandemic will prevent mistakes.

Like a Rorschach inkblot test, merely mention college students and our first thoughts are of boisterous parties, out-of-control drinking and a "what, me worry?" attitude. Who would suspect that this healthy, invincible age group would also be the primary target of the avian flu, ominously poised on the horizon?

"The 1918 flu attacked younger people," says Alan Bova, risk management director at Cornell University in Ithaca,

Susan Gurevitz, "Avian.Flu@edu," *Risk & Insurance*, vol. 17, April 15, 2006, pp. 54–55. Copyright 2006 © LRP Publications. Reproduced by permission.

N.Y., and author of a white paper on the official pandemic response by the University Risk Management and Insurance Association [URMIA] trade group.

People as young as 15 and up to age 40—not the usual vulnerable flu population—made up the bulk of the 675,000 people killed in the United States by the 1918 Spanish flu, the last major flu pandemic.

"It was not the flu itself but the body's powerful overreaction to the flu that wracked those with strong immune systems more than those with weak ones. . . . Paradoxically, the Spanish flu caused the healthiest humans' own immune reactions to kill them," Bova writes in the URMIA report. The avian flu that has already [as of April 2006] sickened more than 184 people in Asia, Europe and Africa is predicted to be even more deadly.

The nature of the universities makes them more vulnerable.

Breeding Grounds for Flu

Exacerbating the situation, college campuses act like giant petri dishes, with students living so close to each other in dorms, sitting in classrooms and eating in dining halls.

"It's the movement, the visitors, the close proximity, so much coming and going from sports teams, admissions tours, visiting scholars and so many other activities," says Janice Abraham, president and CEO of United Educators. Other complicating factors include student and faculty international travel and a campus accessible to the surrounding community. "Thinking about this has got to be on everybody's radar screens," she says.

Maybe it's not on everybody's screens yet, but a number of higher-education insurance brokers, university health officials and risk management people are dusting off any kind of emergency preparedness plans and business continuity strategies they have so they won't be left at the starting gate when the first U.S. cases are reported.

"The big question is how fast can they get their arms around this," says James Graves, vice president for Marsh Risk Consulting in Dallas. "There needs to be a huge sense of urgency for the education industry, especially with what they're seeing on the news. The nature of the universities makes them more vulnerable."

That's why A.J. Gallagher Risk Management Services' Higher Education Group in January [2006] convened a blue-ribbon group of risk managers and public health and Centers for Disease Control and Prevention [CDC] officials to hammer out a 50-page document titled the "Blueprint for Pandemic Flu Preparedness Planning for Colleges and Universities," which Gallagher is distributing to its clients.

Planning for Flu

"Our goal is to provide a benchmark list that institutions should consider," says John E. Watson, executive director, Higher Education Practice Group in Gallagher's Glendale, Calif., office. "Like prior to Sept. 11, 2001, no one ever thought a high-rise office tower could be destroyed, but now that that has happened, people now have to acknowledge that it can occur," he explains. "The same can be said for [hurricanes] Katrina and Rita. This (the avian flu) could also be a catastrophic issue," he says.

The Gallagher blueprint sketches out scenarios of what could happen should a pandemic occur, and then gives an extensive preparedness checklist that schools can follow to set up their own disaster plans. Presented in an outline format, the exhaustive lists of risk assessments, monitoring and campus considerations probably cover most every operation, situation, facility and issue that could surface in an emergency.

Watson acknowledges that it could take as long as an entire academic year to completely refine such a comprehensive emergency plan, "but if you aggressively attack it right now, there's enough in the outline format so in the fall (2006), you'll be able to take advantage of the timing, when all (new students, faculty and staff) are receptive to hearing about new knowledge and information," Watson says.

By the fall [2006], it's quite possible that parents of new students may already start asking about the school's pandemic plan, along with the typical safety questions. In fact, [in] September [2005] students and faculty members at Carnegie Mellon University already started asking for Tamiflu, the six-year-old antiviral prescription drug that's expected to be effective against the current strain of avian flu, but is in short supply.

Carnegie Mellon [University]'s emergency preparedness plan is based upon the strategy developed after September 11.

Apparently at Carnegie Mellon—where international students make up 25 percent of the entire student body—they were even ahead of most public acknowledgment that there was any perceived problem at all.

"I started checking with other schools and went on the listserv to see if anyone else was planning for this because the bird flu overseas was in the media, and very few were even thinking about it," recalls Dr. Anita Barkin, director of the Carnegie Mellon University Student Health Service.

Carnegie Mellon's Plan

Carnegie Mellon's emergency preparedness plan is based upon the strategy developed after Sept. 11, [2001,] in terms of identifying who are the decision-makers, who has which role and responsibility, and how the emergency progresses as it evolves.

"In October (2005), we started pulling work groups together," she says, and in mid-March, they ran a "table-top" drill that went quite smoothly. Barkin's Avian Influenza Response plan identifies 18 different departments, individuals and locations—all considered essential services—laid out on a grid that includes responses broken down on three levels and built upon each other: Level One is for preplanning until the first human transmission case is reported; Level Two kicks in when suspected cases on campus or in the community are reported; and Level Three is reached when confirmed cases on campus are identified.

For example, the first identified group is the "Assessment Team," which is composed of the Facility Management Services, the Environmental Health & Safety department, the Student Health Center and University Police.

Barkin, as the director of the Student Health Center, serves as the incident commander, and "monitoring the situation" and "bringing in housing/dining for quarantine planning" are among her initial Level One duties. Level Two adds "essential personnel receive N95 respirators from the EH&S [Environment, Health & Safety]."

She also recommends training at least two additional people to do the jobs of each essential person in case the frontline people get sick.

Word of her extensive planning document has spread. "I've been inundated with requests for the plan, with well over 200 schools contacting me, including two requests from Canada," says Barkin, who also serves as chairwoman of the Task Force for Pandemic Planning for the American College Health Association. And well they should be contacting her because the health and the safety of the surrounding community, as well as the campus community, are at risk.

If you're not prepared, "what do you do if the CDC says, do this now?" asks Abraham of United Educators.

Contingency Planning

Universities should focus on contingency planning. Should the school continue to operate or should it shut down? Should you send the students home?

"Likely what we'll do is certainly close, if we have the opportunity," says Bova. "That will be one thing we'll be focused on, but we would still have a fairly large population who couldn't go home," he says, referring to the international students.

Marsh's Graves points to supply chain, food services and power as important considerations.

Battling the threat of an avian virus is also an opportunity for colleges and universities to brush up on their business continuity plans. Like contingency planning, continuity plans must address issues such as: How long might the school be shut down—a month, longer or only two to three weeks? How long can the school operate, especially if the personnel who typically operate the campus utilities—water, electricity, phone services—are unavailable?

"Somebody has to know how to turn on the switches," says Gallagher's Watson.

What about tuition—will you still charge it, or refund it? "You may not be able to operate, but are you still going to charge students for living at the school when it's not open?" asks Bova.

By thinking through [the] issues ahead of time, you stand a better chance of being prepared for a pandemic.

Online courses might be a long-term solution, but, as Bova points out, "it takes too long and many resources to develop a course." And there's another unknown—a school's response will depend upon when in the semester the disaster hits.

Liability Risks

The liability risks to higher-education institutions make every risk manager cringe. "If you fail in contingency planning, and if the campus community is not prepared, the university could be held responsible," says Abraham. You don't want to look at your preparedness planning in hindsight, comparing your strategies with better practices of other schools. "If you find yourself sued, when you have to go before the judge and jury, what statements do you want them to be asking—how come your institution didn't do something?" asks Watson.

By thinking through these issues ahead of time, you stand a better chance of being prepared for a pandemic. "When you're ad-libbing, that's when you find yourself making serious mistakes," says Watson.

Abraham adds that there is no business-interruption insurance available for any school to buy for this kind of disaster. "The interruption has to be caused by a covered event, and a pandemic is not a covered event," she says. So get to work on your preparedness plan. Just wash your hands first.

5

Computers Can Predict and Prevent Epidemics

Kim Krisberg

Kim Krisberg is a senior editor at The Nation's Health, *the journal of the American Public Health Association.*

Technology assists public health workers in their fight against disease. Computer users are actively participating by joining the World Community Grid and donating computer time to projects such as finding a cure for dengue or AIDS. Computer modeling also helps public health workers track and predict epidemics so that first responders have the information they need to intervene quickly and effectively. Finally, online computer games have unexpectedly provided insight into how real people might act in the event of a pandemic.

For much of the planet, computers are as ubiquitous to modern life as automobiles and telephones. Whether it's a sleek new laptop or the small chip inside a cell phone, the power of computers has truly changed the world, making it bigger and smaller at the same time. Still, it isn't often that average computer users can boast that their computers are helping to save lives and fight infectious disease.

Launched in 2004, the World Community Grid is in the process of creating the world's largest public computing grid open only to public and nonprofit organizations working on projects that benefit all of humanity. The grid's power source

Kim Krisberg, "Infectious Disease Fight Being Waged in Bits, Bytes: Computers Increasingly Used to Track, Predict, and Prevent Disease," *The Nation's Health*, vol. 37, November 2007, pp. 1–2. Copyright © 2007 The Nation's Health. Reproduced by permission.

isn't a few massive supercomputers tucked away in a laboratory, but hundreds of thousands of everyday computer users who decide to join and add the strength of their computers to the larger collective.

The kinds of calculations that the dengue project is conducting would normally take thousands of years of computer time, but with the World Community Grid, computing through millions of compounds should be done within nine to 12 months.

To join the grid, which is built, supported and maintained by IBM [International Business Machines Corporation], all a person has to do is become a member and download software onto her or his computer. The downloaded software kicks in when a computer is left idle, requesting data from a specific project, performing computations and sending the information back to the main server. As of late September [2007], the grid had almost 330,000 members—donating time from about 750,000 computing devices—and since its launch has generated the equivalent of 114,176 years of computations.

Fighting Disease with Computers

Stan Watowich, PhD, lead researcher and associate professor of biochemistry at the University of Texas Medical Branch, is hoping grid members choose his new infectious disease project to donate their computers' time to. "Discovering Dengue Drugs—Together," which began in August [2007], is using the computational power of the grid to discover treatments for dengue fever, West Nile encephalitis, hepatitis C and yellow fever viruses. Watowich and his colleagues are searching for compounds that inhibit the viruses from replicating. Using the structure of a protein necessary for replication, the dengue project asks idle computers to test whether [any of] millions of drug compounds bind tightly enough to stop the protein from replicating. The grid will then send back a list of compounds most likely to succeed, which researchers can begin testing in a laboratory.

"We've been computing for a few weeks now and received the equivalent of 700 years of computer time already and we're hoping to get up into the tens of thousands of years of computer time," Watowich told *The Nation's Health.*

Watowich said they've already found some compounds that inhibit virus replication in cell culture for both dengue and West Nile virus and will soon be moving those compounds into animal testing. The kinds of calculations that the dengue project is conducting would normally take thousands of years of computer time, but with the World Community Grid, computing through millions of compounds should be done within nine months to 12 months. Nevertheless, there is still much the researchers don't understand, Watowich said, adding that there is a "long road ahead of us."

"Finding treatments that work is just the beginning," he said. "We have to make sure they're safe and affordable for countries that are affected. . . . Many countries in the developing world can't afford drugs and we hope that using resources (such as the World Community Grid) will lower the ultimate cost related to discovery efforts."

Garrett Morris, DPhil., a staff scientist at Scripps Research Institute in La Jolla, Calif., jokingly called the grid a "massive beast that we feed with calculations." Morris works on FightAIDS@Home, which has been using the World Community Grid since 2005 to target the HIV protease, which when effectively blocked prevents the virus from maturing and could eventually prevent the onset of AIDS. In fact, the AIDS project predates the World Community Grid, as it started in 2000 as the first biomedical Internet-based grid computing project at a company called Entropia. Since FightAIDS@Home began working with the global grid [in 2005], 53,000 years worth of calculations have been done, Morris told *The Nation's Health.*

"The scale of this work is unprecedented," he said. "It's truly amazing what we can do."

Researchers have ... been able to predict the way pandemic flu would spread city-by-city and day-by-day during a future flu pandemic in the United States.

Predicting Epidemics

Even though computers seem to get more complicated and savvy every day, diseases can seem savvier—mutating, readapting and evolving to survive based on instinctive programming that's exponentially harder to break than the average computer code. However, advances in computer modeling can now help public health workers stay one step ahead.

Since 2004 at the U.S. National Institute of General Medical Sciences, researchers with the Models of Infectious Disease Agent Study, known as MIDAS, have been constructing computational models of infectious disease outbreaks that can help first responders effectively target disease interventions. Highly complex, the models may take into account every person in the United States, run for weeks at a time and produce millions of different outcomes. While the study collective has a number of research teams—focusing on issues such as cholera, multi-drug resistant tuberculosis and West Nile virus—its work on pandemic flu modeling has had the largest policy impact, according to Irene Eckstrand, PhD, MIDAS' scientific director.

Among the outcomes of the computational research are findings that showed that avian flu was spread human-to-human during a 2006 outbreak in Indonesia and that social distancing played a protective role during the 1918 flu pandemic. Researchers have also been able to predict the way pandemic flu would spread city-by-city and day-by-day during a future flu pandemic in the United States.

"We couldn't build a good model unless we had collaborators who worked with these diseases—experience is critical," Eckstrand told *The Nation's Health.* "Modeling can help us run experiments you could never run on a human population. It might not tell you the on-the-ground truth, but it will show you trends and opportunities you might not otherwise see."

In collaboration with federal health officials, work on pandemic flu modeling has factored significantly into national pandemic planning, Eckstrand said. One day, Eckstrand said she hopes modeling techniques can be widely used at the local level to help health workers predict and control all kinds of disease outbreaks, from mumps to foodborne illness—but she said "we're far from that point."

"We're just on the cutting edge with a long road ahead," Eckstrand said.

The TranStat Computer Model

However, one computer modeling program developed under the MIDAS umbrella is now available free. Developed as a result of the first study to confirm limited human-to-human transmission of avian flu, TranStat allows first responders to enter, save and perform real-time analysis of data from an infectious disease outbreak. The program builds an epidemic curve for users, estimates a real-time fatality rate and determines whether a disease is spreading from person-to-person or whether people are being infected by a common source, according to Ira Longini, PhD, a professor of biostatistics at Seattle's Fred Hutchinson Cancer Research Center and the University of Washington and senior author of the avian flu study. Using disease onset and incubation times, TranStat can help determine if an outbreak is spreading person-to-person, and if so, can tell users how fast the disease is spreading, whether it's being spread through close or casual contact and determine how interventions would affect infection rates, Longini said.

Already, Longini said, he has received numerous requests—mostly from health agencies—asking for TranStat, which can be used to examine other infectious diseases besides flu. He said he's looking forward to getting TranStat "out into the field" as well as receiving feedback that can be used during the creation of TranStat II.

A programming error in World of Warcraft *... turned into a full-blown disease epidemic in 2005, providing a highly realistic glimpse into how people would truly react during a real-world outbreak.*

"Many of the basic questions (public health workers) need to answer fast ... this will help them answer them," Longini said. "We realize it's really the speed of the intervention that's critical.". . .

Computer Game Mirrors Epidemic

It turns out humans aren't the only ones susceptible to an infectious disease outbreak.

A programming error in *World of Warcraft*, an online game with 4 million players worldwide, turned into a full-blown disease epidemic in 2005, providing a highly realistic glimpse into how people would truly react during a real-world outbreak. Unlike computer models, which can't predict the full range of human behavior, game characters mimicked the behavior of their human players. And because the outbreak was completely unintentional on the part of the programmers, the disease's spread mirrored a real epidemiological event, according to Nina Fefferman, PhD, a mathematical epidemiologist who co-authored a study on the virtual outbreak published in the September issue of the *Lancet*.

The outbreak began when the game began allowing higher-level players access to an area where they encountered a character who had the power to infect others with "corrupted blood." According to the study, corrupted blood posed only a minor health threat to powerful players; however, a gamewide epidemic began after a number of infected characters moved to populated areas before being killed or cured.

Even more interesting than the disease's spread was the reaction of the players, Fefferman said. Some players who were safe from corrupted blood moved toward epidemic centers out of curiosity—a behavior real-life epidemiologists don't take into account, she said. Also, characters with healing powers—mimicking the probable behavior of first responders—moved toward the epidemic to help people, becoming infected themselves and spreading the disease even further.

"This is a great experimental set-up, especially for mathematical epidemiologists, who usually take human behavior as a given," she said.

In the end, game programmers were unable to contain the outbreak, but had one weapon in their arsenal that public health workers don't: resetting the game.

6

Travelers Risk Contracting Infectious Diseases

Jakki May

Jakki May writes for the Post Magazine, *a publication that specializes in insurance news.*

Infectious disease is a real threat to the many tourists who visit tropical countries and fail to get the recommended vaccinations—largely out of ignorance—before taking their trips. In addition, although malaria is a devastating disease and rapidly spreading, travelers often do not take antimalarial medicine. As a result, many people either get sick abroad or return home and fall ill. Some insurance companies will not cover expenses incurred as the result of disease if the victim has not taken proper precautions while traveling, including preventive medicine and inoculations.

Mention malaria and many expatriates are likely to shudder in their boots at the very thought of it. But a frightening number of people remain ignorant to the threat of a disease that puts a staggering 40% of the world's population at risk, according to the World Health Organisation [WHO].

Its latest figures show that of the 2.5 billion people at risk, more than 500 million become severely ill with malaria every year and more than one million die from the effects of the disease.

The WHO warns: "Malaria is a particularly serious problem in Africa, where one in every five (20%) childhood deaths

Jakki May, "Repatriation: Malaria—Sleeping with the Enemy," *Post Magazine*, December 20, 2007. © Incisive Media Ltd. 2008. Reproduced by permission.

is due to the effects of the disease. An African child has on average between 1.6 and 5.4 episodes of malaria fever each year. And every 30 seconds a child dies from malaria."

Despite the ease of contracting malaria, one in four [tourists] who did not take malaria drugs did so because they felt they would not catch malaria.

However, while malaria is mostly associated with Africa, it is also found in many other parts of the world, including, increasingly, places like Goa [India] and the Caribbean where many thousands of . . . tourists visit each year. And for many who travel to these areas, there is total ignorance of the risk. A survey conducted by Direct Line [an insurance company] reveals that some three million Britons have visited tropical countries on holiday [between 2002 and 2007] without taking the recommended vaccinations.

It showed that 10% of Britons who visited destinations where the disease is prevalent in [those] five years did not take anti-malaria pills, with a further 8% stopping taking them while still in the infected country. Chris Price, head of travel insurance at Direct Line says that once it drilled down into the research, it uncovered what appears to be widespread ignorance of the necessity of taking medical precautions when visiting tropical countries.

Travelers Ignoring Risks

The research found 17% of people who did not have vaccinations were unaware that they were needed in the first place, with a similar proportion (15%) failing to research what precautions they should take. And despite the ease of contracting malaria, one in four holidaymakers who did not take malaria drugs did so because they felt they would not catch malaria (25%).

Mr Price warns that travellers are far too complacent, with one in five holidaymakers who did not take their vaccinations admitting that they decided to take their chances (21%). One in six (16%) felt that there was no point taking medication because of the brevity of their visit.

He is amazed that "more than half of them are in some sort of state of denial." And it's not just novice travellers who are taking risks. One in five people who did not take medication claimed to be experienced travellers and, therefore, knew how to avoid becoming ill (19%).

The survey did not separate out business from leisure travellers, but Mr Price did question what companies were doing, if they were allowing their employees to jet off around the world without either the necessary information about the risks—or without proper medications. And it seems a high number—around 10%—are not buying insurance even though they are travelling to high risk areas, according to Mr Price.

One surprise to emerge from the survey is that it is not just the young or students who are travelling without insurance, but that it is a problem across all age ranges. And the second surprise was that travellers to far-flung high-risk zones were just as likely not to bother with insurance cover as those going to 'safe' destinations.

False Sense of Security

Mr Price questions whether some of the problems lie in the type of holiday taken. "There are so many holidays where travellers stay in an all-inclusive resort and really do not leave the compound.

"They go straight from the airport to the resort and all their drinks and meals are provided on site. I wonder if that makes them feel safe and if it lulls them into a false sense of security."

But despite that, if people do fall ill in a tropical country, the majority say they would prefer to be brought home for treatment (56%).

Mr Price says: "According to the Department of Health, almost 2000 people return to the UK with malaria each year, and an average of nine people die from the disease." Despite these figures, he says the insurer has yet to insist that travellers take the necessary preventative medication before it will settle a claim.

And it seems that the assistance firms are also able to help the majority of those affected without a problem. Dr Craig Stark, UK medical director for International SOS, says the firm carries out some 15,000 medical evacuations a year and out of the 900 air ambulance cases from Africa "a significant proportion are down to malaria". And the country from which most patients are evacuated is Nigeria—a country where malaria is extremely common.

Malaria Is Preventable

He says the biggest risks to travellers include injuries from some kind of accident, cardiovascular problems and infectious disease—which includes malaria. It staggers him that the assistance firm sees any such cases at all, given that malaria is an entirely preventable disease. "Malaria is preventable and curable so having even one air ambulance a year is unacceptable," he says.

Paul Everett, sales and client services director, Europ Assistance, echoes this: "Malaria is a devastating disease yet it can be prevented and cured if proper steps are taken early. We have had customers who have become ill after deciding not to take Malaria prophylaxis because they have experienced unpleasant side effects.

"We are very conscious, when dealing with cases in areas where malaria is known to be rife, that malaria is always considered first as a possible cause of illness when symptoms are displayed and that the appropriate advice and action is taken."

People [who were] traveling to the [Caribbean] a decade ago may not realise the situation has changed and that they now need protection [from malaria].

Education is the key, according to Mr Stark, but the problem lies in the fact that, for the most part, seeking information is an elective decision. And even if a traveller does try to ask questions, they do not necessarily ask the right people.

"GPs [general practice doctors] may not know the latest information, nor may travel agents. Travellers really need to find sources with up-to-date travel advice."

He points to the re-emergence of the disease in parts of the Caribbean as an example. People [who were] travelling to the area a decade ago may not realise that the situation has changed and that they now need protection.

Picking up Mr Price's point about companies sending employees into at-risk areas, Mr Stark says they do see increasing amounts of effort being made by firms.

"In an age of corporate manslaughter laws, companies have a responsibility to their employees. It is an area we are heavily involved with. By having good education, there is a significant decrease in risk."

Malaria and the Traveler

Mr Stark explains that there are four types of malaria—one of which is particularly severe. Malaria is caused by a parasite called Plasmodium, which is transmitted via the bites of infected mosquitoes. If not treated, malaria can quickly become life threatening. It also needs to be treated in different ways according to the patient. Mr Stark explains that visitors to a malaria-prone area will not have the resistance that local people have developed—in effect they are like children.

As a result, the malaria will need a more aggressive treatment—something that is often hard to do in remote locations—so more visitors will need evacuation than perhaps the local population would require.

"If you took a 30-year-old man from the UK and a 30-year-old man from Nigeria and exposed them to the same malarial disease, the UK man has a significantly higher risk of mortality as he will not have the same ability to fight off the initial infection. The treatment will be different too," Mr Stark adds.

"Because the treatment will be different, the patient often needs to be taken to an area where they can offer that different treatment, so more travellers need to be evacuated."

But Mr Stark says it is also important that travellers discuss exactly where they are going with a medical travel expert. Different areas require different preventative medications because in some areas, the disease has become resistant to certain drugs. This is an issue for travel insurers if they are refusing claims on the grounds that travellers should have taken medication.

Travelers Must Take Medication

Paul Wells, technical claims manager, travel, at Norwich Union [NU], explains: "We exclude claims for tropical diseases where a holidaymaker hasn't taken the recommended medication or had the correct inoculations.

"This is because insurers obviously expect customers to take reasonable care and precautions when travelling to a high risk area. However, it is still possible to contract diseases like malaria even when the right action has been taken prior and during the trip."

As a result, NU will pay out on those claims, as Mr Wells says: "We see around a handful of malaria cases every year which we obviously treat as valid claims. Despite the fact that people are travelling to more exotic climes these days we haven't seen any real increases in claims."

Unlike the others who believe there is much more education to do, he believes: "This is probably down to the travelling public being very aware about what is needed when they go to malaria zones like areas in Africa or India and the information that health and GP services give is generally good and very proactive."

He also adds: "On the whole, if caught early, malaria is treatable with prescription drugs. Problems arise when early symptoms such as fever and flu-like illness (including shaking, chills, headache, muscle aches and tiredness) are not diagnosed. The disease that's left then begins to attack major organs and becomes much more serious and difficult to tackle."

One of the reasons Mr Price believes the official malaria figures are relatively low is the delayed onset of the disease. "People may well have returned home, particularly from a short business trip before they suffer symptoms. Also the symptoms can be hard to spot early on because they are just like flu.

"We think that a good number of cases are handled by the NHS [National Health Service] rather than becoming claims because the traveller has arrived home before becoming sick."

But for those who do get sick abroad, Mr Stark says the cost of repatriation is often high, not least because they need to be evacuated from remote parts of the world. "They need to be evacuated because they need different treatment but the local infrastructure is often not good so the costs go up."

Expatriates Also at Risk

Malaria is not just an issue for occasional travellers, however. Mr Stark warns that expatriates can often be far too complacent about prevention. They see local people—often those they work with—not bothering with any preventative medicine. They then think they can afford to stop taking medication.

"But without that in-built immunity, they are at higher risk," he warns and adds that there is a lot companies can do to help educate their staff. International SOS has developed an online guide, designed to educate travellers before they go. While available to companies, Mr Stark acknowledges it is hard to ensure travellers follow the advice—or even check the site.

The general population is becoming "more and more blasé about overseas travel."

But he says companies should be proactively encouraging their staff to seek expert advice. "Of the four types of malaria, only one is fatal and of those who contract this type, 1% will die.

"One in 100 may sound low but if a company has 1000 employees working overseas, that could mean 10 of them will die. This is an unacceptable risk on something that is preventable," he reiterates.

A worrying statistic to come out of the Direct Line survey is that around 15% of travellers will not even bother to research the risks, according to Mr Price. He wonders whether this is because the general population is becoming "more and more blasé" about overseas travel, with destinations like Bali and Goa becoming routine.

He is sure responsible travel agents and tour operators are advising clients to check with medical experts before travelling, "but if it is happening, it is not happening enough". Direct Line has supported the Association of British Insurers' *Know Before You Go* campaign, which was run in conjunction with the Foreign and Commonwealth Office [FCO]. And Mr Price also suggests travellers check with the FCO site as a matter of routine before travel.

But for the moment, it will be up to individuals to take responsibility and not expose themselves to the double risk of catching the disease and then finding they have one of the policies that will not pay out.

7

Airports Can Handle the Threat of Passenger-Borne Infectious Diseases

Thomas P. Nolan

Thomas P. Nolan is the manager of the Palm Springs International Airport in Palm Springs, California. At the time of writing the following viewpoint he was the assistant director of airports in Wichita, Kansas.

In 2003, a commercial flight scheduled to land in Wichita, Kansas, reported three sick passengers on board who seemed to be suffering from the highly dangerous and infectious SARS (severe acute respiratory syndrome). Airport officials, the local health department, and emergency medical personnel worked together to handle the emergency efficiently and competently. Although the passengers turned out not to have SARS, the situation motivated the airport safety division to develop a written procedure to address future infectious disease emergencies.

There's a lot of discussion regarding airports and how potential aircraft infectious disease situations could mandate that airports maintain sufficient areas to quarantine passengers. Although the discussion appears to be more focused on the large U.S. international gateway airports, other airports might want to consider instituting a plan in case some infectious scenario drops out of the sky. Such a situation occurred at Wichita Mid-Continent Airport (ICT) in 2003, when SARS (Severe Acute Respiratory Syndrome) had the world on edge.

Thomas P. Nolan, "Red Alert: This Is No Drill: As Airports Face the Bird Flu Threat, Wichita Manager Relates One 'Quarantine' Experience," *Airport Business*, vol. 20, no. 7, June 2006, pp. 30–31. Copyright © 2006 Cygnus Business Media. All rights reserved. Reproduced by permission.

Located in Wichita, KS (just about dead center of the U.S.), Mid-Continent Airport handles some 1.5 million passengers annually with direct non-stop airline service to about a dozen major cities, all of which provide international connections. Due to its prime mid-US location, ICT has for years been a convenient diversion point for just about every type of aircraft. Most diversions typically involved circumstances related to aircraft mechanical problems and in-flight passenger medical emergencies.

Our experience, much to our surprise, was not a diverted flight but instead a daily scheduled domestic air carrier flight from a city within 500 miles of Wichita. Fortunately it was mid-week when management and other supervisory personnel were all on hand. That was very relevant because the cumulative experience of all the airport's management team included aircraft accidents and crashes, fires and electrical outages, bomb threats and security incidents, picketing and parking overflow, crippling winter storms and natural disasters—you name it—but never a situation where infectious disease was the center of attention.

A Dangerous Situation

On that day, the scheduled commercial CRJ [Canadair Regional Jet] captain discovered, half-way into the hour-long flight, three passengers of Asian descent exhibiting signs of the then-popular SARS. The captain subsequently radioed his corporate operations center to report the situation (consistent with the airline's newly established procedures); then someone from airline operations called our airport's safety division to advise us of the situation and need for attention. It was this phonecall from the airline that officially handed the baton to the airport. We then knew it was going to be our event to manage, regardless of whether or not we were prepared.

Faced with the reality that we had an inbound aircraft containing a suspected infectious disease situation, the ICT team assembled to formulate the best plan of attack. We had experience handling serious life-threatening medical diversions; however, not being an international gateway airport, we had never had any reason to have specific procedures for infectious disease situations. We'd provided staff with appropriate training and procedures for handling of materials and patients related to the control of bloodborne pathogens, but it's not the same animal—SARS could be transmitted via airborne particles.

With only minutes to make key decisions and formulate a plan, all kinds of questions popped up. Where is the best place to stage the aircraft? What to do with the other passengers once the suspected SARS individuals were isolated? What about the crew, the aircraft, the terminal? Should we allow any passengers to enter the building? If we do, should we shut the ventilation down to minimize the circulation of airborne particles? If we have no choice but to deplane in the terminal, do we have to drench the building in bleach and antibacterial spray to try and make the interior air safe once more once the passengers leave? What about all the other people in the building? How do we address the liability issues? Will we be forced to shut down the terminal for days and essentially put ourselves and airline tenants out of business?

With county health officials on hand, . . . we had the right decision makers within our midst regarding the disposition of the passengers, crew, and three suspected SARS carriers.

Once the aircraft landed and we made the (correct) decision to keep the local airline management involved, station personnel instructed them to direct the captain that he [was] not to taxi the aircraft up to the passenger boarding bridge, and that there wasn't going to be any deplaning of passengers into the terminal. We asked FAA/ATC [Federal Aviation

Administration/Air Traffic Control] to advise the pilot of this same directive, knowing the conversation would be on a recorded frequency. The captain was instructed not to open the door of the aircraft or to allow anyone to deplane, not even on the ramp, until authorization was given from airport management. The captain complied and parked the aircraft some 100 feet short of the passenger boarding bridge.

Working Together

Our local EMS [emergency medical services] and County Health Department officials were notified sometime shortly after we first learned of the in-flight situation. Officials who never really had reason in the past to [rush] to the airport took some time to arrive. (They were probably as surprised as we were.)

The airport safety division developed an Operating Instruction, an internal written procedure for handling aircraft (scheduled or diverted) with infectious passengers (suspected or verified).

With county health officials on hand, we knew we had the right decision makers within our midst regarding the disposition of the passengers, crew, and three suspected SARS carriers. After being briefed, the officials boarded the aircraft to gain some information from the three individuals; they then authorized the deplaning of passengers. They commended the decision to not allow the captain to deplane anyone. Yet, at this point we still needed somewhere to put the passengers and crew for further attention by health officials.

In order to find a space to "quarantine" the 40 or so individuals, we decided the terminal was off limits, and we were not about to start asking tenants to empty hangars and cease conducting their business. The best solution was to bring the space to the passengers, accomplished by using the airport bus.

The non-SARS-suspected passengers were transferred to the bus where the health department officials checked every passenger. Information gathered from the three suspected SARS passengers indicated that SARS was not the likely culprit. As a precaution, they were isolated in a different vehicle for questioning and then transported by EMS to the local hospital for examination.

Additional Precautions

As another precaution, the baggage was not unloaded onto the normal baggage handling system; instead, passengers were escorted to the front curb and bags were delivered to them. To shield the terminal from any type of airborne contamination, all passengers were asked to not enter the terminal. If they had any airline or rental car issues, personnel from those agencies were brought to the outside. Pages were also made to any meeters and greeters to direct them to the front terminal curb or in the lot. As expected, the media converged on this event, and we kept them informed during the entire situation.

We conducted a post-incident review that included the health department, the airport, and other emergency response personnel. It allowed us to immediately identify some of issues we confronted. During ensuing months, we held similar meetings to develop an actual response plan. The airport safety division developed an Operating Instruction, an internal written procedure for handling aircraft (scheduled or diverted) with infectious disease passengers (suspected or verified).

It was written into our plan that suspect aircraft would never be allowed to deplane into the passenger terminal, or any building for that matter. Aircraft and passengers will be staged on the cargo apron, well away from the terminal, to allow easy staging of personnel and equipment. It was also decided that if local or federal health officials mandated a quarantine on-airport, then either the aircraft itself or buses would be utilized.

8

Vaccinations Prevent Infectious Diseases

Centers for Disease Control and Prevention

The Centers for Disease Control and Prevention (CDC) is a division of the United States Department of Health and Human Services. The CDC is the primary federal agency conducting and supporting public health activities in the United States.

Over the years, vaccines have protected many people from infectious diseases. Without vaccinations, many people would have been disabled or died from diseases such as polio, measles, meningitis, pertussis (whooping cough), pneumonia, rubella, chicken pox, hepatitis B, diphtheria, tetanus, and mumps. The viruses and bacteria that cause these diseases still exist, however, and there would be a dramatic resurgence of these diseases if people stopped getting vaccinated. Therefore, because vaccines have been proven to be safe in most circumstances and because they protect people from deadly and disabling disease, the benefits far outweigh any potential risks.

In the U.S., vaccines have reduced or eliminated many infectious diseases that once routinely killed or harmed many infants, children, and adults. However, the viruses and bacteria that cause vaccine-preventable disease and death still exist and can be passed on to people who are not protected by vaccines. Vaccine-preventable diseases have many social and economic costs: sick children miss school and can cause parents to lose time from work. These diseases also result in doctor's visits, hospitalizations, and even premature deaths.

Centers for Disease Control and Prevention, "What Would Happen If We Stopped Vaccinations?" Centers for Disease Control Web site, June 12, 2007. Information obtained from the Centers for Disease Control (www.cdc.gov).

Before Vaccinations

Stopping vaccination against polio will leave people susceptible to infection with the polio virus. Polio virus causes acute
paralysis that can lead to permanent physical disability and
even death. Before polio vaccine was available, 13,000 to
20,000 cases of paralytic polio were reported each year in the
United States. These annual epidemics of polio often left thousands of victims—mostly children—in braces, crutches, wheel-
chairs, and iron lungs. The effects were life-long.

---

*If vaccinations were stopped, each year about 2.7 million
measles deaths worldwide could be expected.*

In 1988 the World Health Assembly unanimously agreed
to eradicate polio worldwide. As a result of global polio eradication efforts, the number of cases reported globally has decreased from more than 350,000 cases in 125 countries in
1988 to 2,000 cases of polio in 17 countries in 2006, and only
four countries remain endemic (Afghanistan, India, Nigeria,
Pakistan). To date polio has been eliminated from the Western
hemisphere, and the European and Western Pacific regions.
Stopping vaccination before eradication is achieved would result in a resurgence of the disease in the United States and
worldwide.

Before measles immunization was available, nearly everyone in the U.S. got measles. An average of 450 measles-
associated deaths were reported each year between 1953 and
1963.

In the U.S., up to 20 percent of persons with measles are
hospitalized. Seventeen percent of measles cases have had one
or more complications, such as ear infections, pneumonia, or
diarrhea. Pneumonia is present in about six percent of cases
and accounts for most of the measles deaths. Although less

common, some persons with measles develop encephalitis (swelling of the lining of the brain), resulting in brain damage.

As many as three of every 1,000 persons with measles will die in the U.S. In the developing world, the rate is much higher, with death occurring in about one of every 100 persons with measles.

Measles is one of the most infectious diseases in the world and is frequently imported into the U.S. In the period 1997–2000, most cases were associated with international visitors or U.S. residents who were exposed to the measles virus while traveling abroad. More than 90 percent of people who are not immune will get measles if they are exposed to the virus.

According to the World Health Organization (WHO), nearly 900,000 measles-related deaths occurred among persons in developing countries in 1999. In populations that are not immune to measles, measles spreads rapidly. If vaccinations were stopped, each year about 2.7 million measles deaths worldwide could be expected.

In the U.S., widespread use of measles vaccine has led to a greater than 99 percent reduction in measles compared with the pre-vaccine era. If we stopped immunization, measles would increase to pre-vaccine levels.

Before Hib [meningitis-causing bacterium] vaccine became available, Hib was the most common cause of bacterial meningitis in U.S. infants and children. Before the vaccine was developed, there were approximately 20,000 invasive Hib cases annually. Approximately two-thirds of the 20,000 cases were meningitis, and one-third were other life-threatening invasive Hib diseases such as bacteria in the blood, pneumonia, or inflammation of the epiglottis. About one of every 200 U.S. children under 5 years of age got an invasive Hib disease. Hib meningitis once killed 600 children each year and left many survivors with deafness, seizures, or mental retardation.

Since introduction of conjugate Hib vaccine in December 1987, the incidence of Hib has declined by 98 percent. From 1994–1998, fewer than 10 fatal cases of invasive Hib disease were reported each year.

This preventable disease was a common, devastating illness as recently as 1990; now, most pediatricians just finishing training have never seen a case. If we were to stop immunization, we would likely soon return to the pre-vaccine numbers of invasive Hib disease cases and deaths. . . .

Chicken Pox Is Preventable

Prior to the licensing of the chickenpox [varicella] vaccine in 1995, almost all persons in the United States had suffered from chickenpox by adulthood. Each year, the virus caused an estimated 4 million cases of chickenpox, 11,000 hospitalizations, and 100–150 deaths.

A highly contagious disease, chickenpox is usually mild but can be severe in some persons. Infants, adolescents and adults, pregnant women, and immunocompromised persons are at particular risk for serious complications including secondary bacterial infections, loss of fluids (dehydration), pneumonia, and central nervous system involvement. The availability of the chickenpox vaccine and its subsequent widespread use has had a major impact on reducing cases of chickenpox and related morbidity, hospitalizations, and deaths. In some areas, cases have decreased as much as 90 percent over prevaccination numbers.

In 2006, routine two-dose vaccination against chickenpox was recommended for all children, adolescents, and adults who do not have evidence of immunity to the disease. In addition to further reducing cases, this strategy will also decrease the risk for exposure to the virus for persons who are unable to be vaccinated because of illness or other conditions and who may develop severe disease. If vaccination against chickenpox were to stop, the disease would eventually return to prevaccination rates, with virtually all susceptible persons becoming infected with the virus at some point in their lives.

Infants and children who become infected with hepatitis B virus are at highest risk of developing lifelong infection.

Hepatitis B Risk Reduced

More than 2 billion persons worldwide have been infected with the hepatitis B virus at some time in their lives. Of these, 350 million are life-long carriers of the disease and can transmit the virus to others. One million of these people die each year from liver disease and liver cancer.

National studies have shown that about 12.5 million Americans have been infected with hepatitis B virus at some point in their lifetime. One and one quarter million Americans are estimated to have chronic (long-lasting) infection, of whom 20 percent to 30 percent acquired their infection in childhood. Chronic hepatitis B virus infection increases a person's risk for chronic liver disease, cirrhosis, and liver cancer. About 5,000 persons will die each year from hepatitis B–related liver disease resulting in over $700 million in medical and work loss costs.

The number of new infections per year has declined from an average of 450,000 in the 1980s to about 80,000 in 1999. The greatest decline has occurred among children and adolescents due to routine hepatitis B vaccination.

Infants and children who become infected with hepatitis B virus are at highest risk of developing lifelong infection, which often leads to death from liver disease (cirrhosis) and liver cancer. Approximately 25 percent of children who become infected with life-long hepatitis B virus would be expected to die of related liver disease as adults.

CDC estimates that one-third of the life-long hepatitis B virus infections in the United States resulted from infections occurring in infants and young children. About 16,000–20,000 hepatitis B antigen–infected women give birth each year in the United States. It is estimated that 12,000 children born to hepatitis B virus–infected mothers were infected each year before implementation of infant immunization programs. In addition, approximately 33,000 children (10 years of age and younger) of mothers who are not infected with hepatitis B virus were infected each year before routine recommendation of childhood hepatitis B vaccination.

The Threat of Diptheria

Diphtheria is a serious disease caused by a bacterium. This germ produces a poisonous substance or toxin which frequently causes heart and nerve problems. The case fatality rate is 5 percent to 10 percent, with higher case-fatality rates (up to 20 percent) in the very young and the elderly.

In the 1920's, diphtheria was a major cause of illness and death for children in the U.S. In 1921, a total of 206,000 cases and 15,520 deaths were reported. With vaccine development in 1923, new cases of diphtheria began to fall in the U.S., until in 2001 only two cases were reported.

Although diphtheria is rare in the U.S., it appears that the bacteria continue to get passed among people. In 1996, 10 isolates of the bacteria were obtained from persons in an American Indian community in South Dakota, none of whom had classic diphtheria disease. There was one death reported in 2003 from clinical diphtheria in a 63-year-old male who had never been vaccinated.

There are high rates of susceptibility among adults. Screening tests conducted since 1977 have shown that 41 percent to 84 percent of adults 60 and over lack protective levels of circulating antitoxin against diphtheria.

Although diphtheria is rare in the U.S., it is still a threat. Diphtheria is common in other parts of the world and with the increase in international travel, diphtheria and other infectious diseases are only a plane ride away. If we stopped immunization, the U.S. might experience a situation similar to the Newly Independent States of the former Soviet Union. With the breakdown of the public health services in this area, diphtheria epidemics began in 1990, fueled primarily by persons who were not properly vaccinated. From 1990–1999, more than 150,000 cases and 5,000 deaths were reported.

Tetanus Kills the Unprotected

Tetanus is a severe, often fatal disease. The bacteria that cause tetanus are widely distributed in soil and street dust, are found in the waste of many animals, and are very resistant to heat and germ-killing cleaners. From 1922—1926, there were an estimated 1,314 cases of tetanus per year in the U.S. In the late 1940's, the tetanus vaccine was introduced, and tetanus became a disease that was officially counted and tracked by public health officials. In 2000, only 41 cases of tetanus were reported in the U.S.

People who get tetanus suffer from stiffness and spasms of the muscles. The larynx (throat) can close causing breathing and eating difficulties, muscles spasms can cause fractures (breaks) of the spine and long bones, and some people go into a coma, and die. Approximately 20 percent of reported cases end in death.

Tetanus in the U.S. is primarily a disease of adults, but unvaccinated children and infants of unvaccinated mothers are also at risk for tetanus and neonatal tetanus, respectively. From 1995–1997, 33 percent of reported cases of tetanus occurred among persons 60 years of age or older and 60 percent occurred in patients greater than 40 years of age. The National Health Interview Survey found that in 1995, only 36 percent of adults 65 or older had received a tetanus vaccination during the preceding 10 years.

Worldwide, tetanus in newborn infants continues to be a huge problem. Every year tetanus kills 300,000 newborns and

30,000 birth mothers who were not properly vaccinated. Even though the number of reported cases is low, an increased number of tetanus cases in younger persons has been observed recently in the U.S. among intravenous drug users, particularly heroin users.

Tetanus is infectious, but not contagious, so unlike other vaccine-preventable diseases, immunization by members of the community will not protect others from the disease. Because tetanus bacteria are widespread in the environment, tetanus can only be prevented by immunization. If vaccination against tetanus were stopped, persons of all ages in the U.S. would be susceptible to this serious disease.

Mumps is highly communicable, and it only takes a few unvaccinated to initiate transmission.

Mumps Outbreaks

Before the mumps vaccine was introduced, mumps was a major cause of deafness in children, occurring in approximately 1 in 20,000 reported cases. Mumps is usually a mild viral disease. However, rare conditions such as swelling of the brain, nerves and spinal cord can lead to serious side effects such as paralysis, seizures, and fluid in the brain.

Serious side effects of mumps are more common among adults than children. Swelling of the testes is the most common side effect in males past the age of puberty, occurring in up to 20 percent to 50 percent of men who contract mumps. An increase in miscarriages has been found among women who develop mumps during the first trimester of pregnancy.

An estimated 212,000 cases of mumps occurred in the U.S. in 1964. After vaccine licensure in 1967, reports of mumps decreased rapidly. In 1986 and 1987, there was a resurgence of mumps with 12,848 cases reported in 1987. Since 1989, the incidence of mumps has declined, with 266 reported cases in

2001. This recent decrease is probably due to the fact that children have received a second dose of mumps vaccine (part of the two-dose schedule for measles, mumps, rubella or MMR) and the eventual development of immunity in those who did not gain protection after the first mumps vaccination.

We cannot let our guard down against mumps. A 2006 outbreak among college students, most of whom had received two doses of vaccine, led to over 5500 cases in 15 states. Mumps is highly communicable, and it only takes a few unvaccinated to initiate transmission.

9

Vaccinations Harm Children

Barbara Loe Fisher

Barbara Loe Fisher is the cofounder and president of the National Vaccine Information Center (NVIC). She has served on the National Vaccine Advisory Committee, the Institute of Medicine Vaccine Safety Forum, and the Food and Drug Administration's Vaccines and Related Biological Products Advisory Committee.

Vaccinations may cause injury to the brains of children and may also be the source of many chronic autoimmune diseases now suffered by American children. There have not been adequate studies to demonstrate the safety of viral and bacterial vaccines when given in combination. In addition, there have been few studies to demonstrate the effects of environmental toxins on vaccines. Finally, some children's genetic makeups may make them particularly prone to dangerous reactions to immunizations.

America and America's children are in the midst of an epidemic of chronic disease and disability. Today, the Centers for Disease Control [and Prevention, the CDC,] admits that one American child in 166 has been diagnosed with autism spectrum disorder. In 1970, autism affected four in 10,000 children. By 1991, 5,000 autistic children were in the public school system; by 2001, that number had grown to 94,000. Today, the CDC reports that 9 million American children under 18 have been diagnosed with asthma. In 1979, asthma affected approximately 2 million children under age 14.5.

Barbara Loe Fisher, "In the Wake of Vaccines," *Mothering: Natural Family Living*, September/October, 2004. Reproduced by permission of the author.

Today, nearly 3 million children in public schools are classified as learning disabled. In 1976, there were 796,000 learning-disabled children in public schools. Today, the CDC reports that 4 million children between the ages of 3 and 17 years have been diagnosed with ADHD [attention-deficit hyperactivity disorder]. The government has only recently begun monitoring the numbers of children with ADHD. In 1997, ADHD was reported to affect about 1.6 million elementary school children.

Today, 206,000 Americans under the age of 20 have type 1 diabetes, while type 2 diabetes is mysteriously on the rise in children and adolescents. The CDC estimates that 1 in 400 to 500 American children and adolescents are now diabetic. Between 1945 and 1969, the incidence of diabetes in children aged 6 to 18 was approximately 1 in 7,100 children.

For more than 100 years, doctors have been publishing articles in the medical literature about the brain-damaging side effects of vaccines.

Today, arthritis affects one in three Americans and about 300,000 American children have juvenile rheumatoid arthritis. Juvenile rheumatoid arthritis used to be so rare that statistics were not kept until its recent rise in children. These brain and immune-system disorders plaguing millions of the most highly vaccinated children in the world are preventing too many of them from thriving, learning, and achieving in the ways past generations of children have thrived, learned, and achieved. And our nation is only beginning to understand the enormous price tag that comes with the burden of chronic disease. In America, the cost of health care for chronic disease is estimated to be $425 billion a year, and it is rising. . . .

A Vaccines–Chronic Disease Link?

It wasn't always like this. What is happening to the health of our nation? Could it have anything to do with exposing our children to more and more bacterial and live virus vaccines in the first five years of life, when the brain and immune system develop most rapidly? And could we be compromising the integrity of our immune systems by eliminating all experience of natural infection?

For more than 100 years, doctors have been publishing articles in the medical literature about the brain-damaging side effects of vaccines. The mother of all vaccines—the smallpox vaccine, created by Britain's Edward Jenner in 1796—was found to cause inflammation of the brain in one in 3,200 persons. After Pasteur began to inject patients with rabies vaccine in the 1880s, it became obvious that brain inflammation was a side effect that affected as many as one in 400 vaccinated persons. And by the 1960s and '70s, the medical literature was full of reports that the pertussis (whooping cough) vaccine was causing brain inflammation and death in babies getting the DPT [diphtheria, pertussis and tetanus] shot.

Doctors and public health officials were talking to each other in the pages of medical journals about the fact that vaccines could injure children's brains, but those being vaccinated had no clue. Mothers taking their children to pediatricians to be vaccinated placed a blind trust in the complete safety and effectiveness of those vaccines.

From Healthy to Sick

I trusted without questioning when I took my newborn to my pediatrician for baby shots in the late 1970s. At the time, I considered myself a woman very well-educated in science and medicine. My mother and grandmother had been nurses, and I had become a medical writer at a teaching hospital after graduating from college.

But I knew nothing about the risks of vaccines, which I assumed were 100 percent safe and effective. It never occurred to me that a medical intervention designed to keep a healthy child healthy could ever harm that child. The concept of risk associated with prevention is quite different from the concept of risk associated with a cure. . . .

The day of his fourth DPT and OPV [oral polio vaccine] shots, when he was two and a half, Chris was healthy except for slight diarrhea left over from a 48-hour bout with the stomach flu he had had at the beach three weeks earlier. He had just come off of a round of antibiotics because, back then, antibiotics were given for everything from flu to pneumonia. The pediatrician, as well as the nurse preparing to give Chris his shots, said he didn't have a fever, and that a little diarrhea didn't matter.

Several hours after we got home, I realized how quiet it was in the house, and went upstairs to look for Chris. I walked into his bedroom to find him sitting in a rocking chair staring straight ahead, as if he couldn't see me standing in the doorway. His face was white and his lips were slightly blue. When I called out his name, his eyelids fluttered, his eyes rolled back in his head, and his head fell to his shoulder. It was as if he had suddenly fallen asleep sitting up.

None of the doctors knew what was wrong with my son, who had become an entirely different child.

This was unusual—I had never before seen him fall asleep while sitting up. When I picked him up and carried him to his bed, he was like a dead weight in my arms. I remember thinking that maybe he was so tired because of what had happened at the doctor's office, or maybe he was having a relapse of the flu. Chris slept in his bed without moving for more than six hours, through dinnertime, until I called my mom, who told me to try to wake him.

I climbed into Chris's bed, lifted his limp body, and cradled his back against my chest as I rocked us both from side to side, calling out his name. I could feel him struggling to awake. He began mumbling the word bathroom, but he couldn't sit up on his own or walk. I picked him up and carried him to the bathroom, where he had severe diarrhea and then, again, fell asleep sitting up. He slept for 12 more hours.

This was 1980. I had been given no information by my doctor about how to recognize a vaccine reaction.

Further Deterioration

In the following days and weeks, Chris deteriorated. He no longer knew his alphabet or numbers, and couldn't identify the cards he once knew so well. He would not look at the books we had once read together every day. He couldn't concentrate for more than a few seconds at a time. My little boy, once so happy-go-lucky, no longer smiled. He was now listless and emotionally fragile, crying or becoming angry at the slightest frustration.

Chris's physical deterioration was just as profound. He had constant diarrhea, stopped eating, stopped growing, and was plagued with respiratory and ear infections for the first time in his life. The pediatrician told me it was just a stage he was going through and not to worry about it. After eight months of such deterioration, I took Chris to another pediatrician. He was tested for cystic fibrosis and celiac disease, but the tests came back negative. None of the doctors knew what was wrong with my son, who had become an entirely different child physically, mentally, and emotionally.

It would be another year before I stood in my kitchen and watched the Emmy Award-winning NBC-TV documentary *DPT: Vaccine Roulette*, produced by consumer reporter Lea Thompson in spring 1982. I called the television station and asked to see the medical research that had been used to document the show. There, in the pages of *Pediatrics, The New England Journal of Medicine, The Lancet,* and *The British Medical Journal,* I found clinical descriptions of reactions to the pertussis vaccine that exactly matched the symptoms I had witnessed my son have within four hours of his fourth DPT shot.

I learned that, in 1981, the British National Childhood Encephalopathy Study had reported a statistically significant correlation between DPT vaccine and brain inflammation leading to chronic neurological damage, and that the UCLA-FDA [University of California, Los Angeles-Food and Drug Administration] study published in *Pediatrics* in 1981 had found that one in 875 DPT shots is followed within 48 hours by a convulsion or collapse/shock reaction just like the one my son had suffered. As I leafed through more than 50 years of medical literature documenting the fact that the complications of pertussis disease, or whooping cough, were identical to the complications of whole-cell pertussis vaccine, I was stunned. I felt betrayed by a medical profession I had revered all my life.

Mothers . . . took healthy, bright children to doctors to be vaccinated and, within hours, days, or weeks, their children got sick, regressed, and became different children.

The day Chris had his vaccine reaction, he should have been in an emergency room, not unconscious in his bed. As his mother, I should have had the information I needed to recognize what was happening to him and take steps to deal with it, including calling my doctor and, later, making sure the reaction was recorded in his medical record and reported to the vaccine manufacturer and health officials.

A Long List of Problems

At age six, when Chris could not learn to read or write, he was given an extensive battery of tests that confirmed minimal brain damage that took the form of multiple learning disabilities, including: fine motor and short-term memory delays; dyslexia; auditory processing deficits; attention deficit disorder; and other developmental delays. He was removed from the Montessori school he attended and placed in a self-contained classroom for the learning-disabled in public school, where he stayed throughout elementary, junior, and high school, despite repeated unsuccessful efforts by the schools to "mainstream" him.

As a teenager, Chris struggled to deal with the big gaps between certain aspects of his intelligence—such as his creativity and his unusual ability to think on an abstract level, mixed with his inability to concentrate for long periods of time or to organize and process certain kinds of information he saw or heard. He was angry and frustrated because he couldn't do what his peers could do, and was troubled both in and out of school. After working in a warehouse and mail room following high school, he eventually earned an associate degree in video and film production at a school where a third of the students are learning disabled and receive in-depth tutorial support. Chris is now making his way in the world using his creative gifts. He continually adjusts for the learning disabilities that will always be a part of who he is, but that he is determined will not define who he is.

Issue Will Not Go Away

My son's vaccine reaction nearly a quarter century ago is identical to those that Harris Coulter and I reported in 1985 in *DPT: A Shot in the Dark,* and those that thousands of other mothers have reported to the National Vaccine Information Center (NVIC) for the past 22 years. These mothers tell us how they took healthy, bright children to doctors to be vaccinated and, within hours, days, or weeks, their children got sick, regressed, and became different children. Whether a child recovers, is left with minimal brain damage as my son was, or is more severely injured—as was the case with the children who were awarded nearly $2 billion in compensation under the National Childhood Vaccine Injury Act of 1986—a pattern of common experience emerges. This pattern, repeated over and over in homes across America, has contributed in no small way to why the issue of vaccine safety will not go away.

Mothers call the NVIC and describe how, within days of vaccination, their babies run fevers; scream for hours, fall into a deep sleep, and wake up screaming again; start twitching, jerking, or staring into space as if they can't hear or see; are covered with body rashes; become restless and irritable; or have a dramatic change in eating or sleeping habits.

Others describe a gradual deterioration in overall health, a picture that includes constant ear and respiratory infections and onset of allergies, including asthma; unexplained rashes; new sensitivity to foods such as milk; persistent diarrhea; sleep disturbances that turn night into day and day into night; loss of developmental milestones such as the ability to roll over or sit up; loss of speech, eye-contact, and communication skills; development of strange or violent behaviors that include hyperactivity, biting, hitting, social withdrawal, and repetitive movements such as flapping, rocking, and head banging. Older children and adults complain of muscle weakness, joint pain, crippling headaches, disabling fatigue, loss of memory, or being unable to concentrate and think clearly.

Has the repeated manipulation of the immune system with multiple vaccines . . . been an unrecognized cofactor in the epidemics of chronic disease and disability plaguing so many children today?

Depending on the child and the specific therapy interventions, there is either gradual full recovery or the child is eventually diagnosed with various kinds of chronic health problems. My son regressed after his DPT shot but stopped just short of autism. Why? I don't know. Vaccine-induced brain injuries appear to be on a continuum ranging from milder forms such as ADD or ADHD and learning disabilities to autism-spectrum and seizure disorders to severe mental retardation, all the way to death. On this continuum, and often coinciding with brain dysfunction, is immune-system dysfunction ranging from development of severe allergies and asthma to intestinal bowel disorders, rheumatoid arthritis, and diabetes. . . .

How Many Injured Children?

But how many children have vaccine reactions every year? Is it really only one in 110,000 or one in a million who are left permanently disabled after vaccination? Former FDA Commissioner David Kessler observed in 1993 that less than 1 percent of doctors report adverse events following prescription drug use. There have been estimates that perhaps less than 5 or 10 percent of doctors report hospitalizations, injuries, deaths, or other serious health problems following vaccination. The 1986 Vaccine Injury Act contained no legal sanctions for not reporting; doctors can refuse to report and suffer no consequences.

Even so, each year about 12,000 reports are made to the Vaccine Adverse Event Reporting System; parents as well as doctors can make those reports. However, if that number represents only 10 percent of what is actually occurring, then the actual number may be 120,000 vaccine-adverse events. If doctors report vaccine reactions as infrequently as Dr. Kessler said they report prescription-drug reactions, and the number 12,000 is only 1 percent of the actual total, then the real number may be 1.2 million vaccine-adverse events annually. The larger unanswered question that haunts every new vaccine mandate is: Has the repeated manipulation of the immune system with multiple vaccines in the first three years of life, when the interrelated brain and immune systems develop most rapidly outside the womb, been an unrecognized cofactor in the epidemics of chronic disease and disability plaguing so many children today?

10

Low Adult Immunization Rates Increase the Risk for Infectious Disease

Jennifer Corrigan

Jennifer Corrigan is a staff writer for the National Foundation of Infectious Diseases.

Although children in the United States are routinely immunized against common illnesses by vaccination, a large number of adults either do not choose to be immunized or are unaware that such vaccinations exist. Diseases such as influenza, shingles, mumps, and tetanus, among others, can be prevented by proper immunization. Because infectious diseases sicken and sometimes kill many Americans each year, adults need to have themselves immunized against diseases for which there are vaccinations available.

Data released [in 2008] by the Centers for Disease Control and Prevention (CDC) paint a disappointing picture of adult immunization against serious infectious diseases in the United States. In addition, a new consumer survey shows the vast majority of adult Americans lack awareness of vaccines and [of] the severity of infectious diseases.

An expert panel discussed the data at a press conference held by the National Foundation for Infectious Diseases (NFID), which called for increased use of vaccines in adults to reduce needless illness and deaths associated with infectious diseases.

Jennifer Corrigan, "New Data Show Unacceptably Low Adult Immunization Rates and That Adults Unaware of Infectious Disease Threat," *US Newswire*, January 23, 2008. Reproduced by permission.

CDC's National Immunization Survey shows only 2.1 percent of adults 18 to 64 years of age are immunized against tetanus-diphtheria-whooping cough. Immunization to prevent shingles among people 60 and over was only 1.9 percent. Vaccine coverage for the prevention of HPV (human papillomavirus) among women 18 to 26 is about 10 percent. In addition, influenza and pneumococcal vaccination rates for the elderly are well below the 90 percent national target rates.

Infectious diseases kill more Americans annually than either breast cancer, HIV/AIDS or traffic accidents.

Vaccinations Prevent Disease

"Routine immunization of children in the United States has saved hundreds of thousands of lives and prevented millions of cases of disease, but vaccines are not just for children," said Anne Schuchat, MD, director of the CDC's National Center for Immunization and Respiratory Diseases. "These new data show there are not yet very many adults taking full advantage of the great advancements in prevention that have been made in the past few years."

"There are now 17 diseases that can be prevented from vaccines given to children, teens and adults. Several vaccines, including three fairly new ones licensed since 2005, are recommended specifically for the adult years. By skipping vaccination, people are leaving themselves needlessly vulnerable to significant illness, long-term suffering and even death," said Dr. Schuchat. "We are extremely fortunate in this country to have safe and effective vaccines available, but we have to use them better."

Immunization is recommended for U.S. adults to protect them against chickenpox, diphtheria, hepatitis A, hepatitis B, human papillomavirus/cervical cancer (HPV), influenza, measles, meningococcal disease, mumps, pertussis (whooping cough), pneumococcal disease, rubella, shingles and tetanus.

"Combined, these infectious diseases kill more Americans annually than either breast cancer, HIV/AIDS or traffic accidents," said William Schaffner, MD, Vice President of NFID and Chairman of the Department of Preventive Medicine at Vanderbilt University School of Medicine.

"A concerted effort is needed to raise adult immunization rates," said Dr. Schaffner. "The important thing to remember is that deaths and illness associated with these infections are largely avoidable through vaccination."

Adults Unaware of Vaccines

Also released were results of a national survey conducted by NFID that show most adults cannot name more than one or two diseases that are vaccine preventable in adults. Each vaccine for adults was identified by only 3 to 18 percent of those polled; the only exception was the influenza vaccine, which was named by just under half of respondents.

Also disconcerting is that half of those surveyed say they are not concerned about whether they or another adult family member gets a vaccine-preventable disease. When asked about specific diseases, consumers expressed most concern about getting influenza, which likely reflects the more frequent messages they receive about influenza versus the other diseases.

One adult vaccine with low immunization rates ([less than] 2 percent) prevents herpes zoster, or shingles, a severely painful and debilitating infectious disease. "There are more than 1 million new cases of shingles in the U.S. every year; over half in people 60 and older," said Michael N. Oxman, MD, Professor, University of California, San Diego; Staff Physician at the San Diego VA [Veterans Administration] Medical Center; and Chairman of the Shingles Prevention Study, the VA Cooperative Study that demonstrated the efficacy of the shingles vaccine. "The vaccine not only helps reduce the risk of getting shingles, but it reduces the incidence of postherpetic neuralgia (PHN), a long-lasting shingles pain syndrome that constitutes the most common serious and debilitating complication of shingles." PHN pain can last for years after the initial shingles outbreak and is often resistant to treatment.

Stanley A. Gall, MD, Professor of Obstetrics, Gynecology and Women's Health and the American College of Obstetricians and Gynecologists (ACOG) Liaison Member to the Advisory Committee on Immunization Practices, addressed the importance of using the HPV vaccine to protect women against human papillomavirus. "The 2007 reported coverage rate of 10 percent in women 18 to 26 is a start, but we need to get these rates up. This is a safe and effective vaccine that protects against cervical cancer. I urge all young women to talk to their doctors about getting the three-dose vaccine series."

Although immunization rates are higher for influenza than for other vaccines recommended for adults, "influenza remains a significant threat to the public health," according to Kristin L. Nichol, MD, MPH, MBA, Chief of Medicine, Minneapolis VA Medical Center and Professor of Medicine and Vice Chair, Department of Medicine, University of Minnesota. "We are learning more all the time about just how severe, debilitating and widespread influenza can be. A recent report connected influenza infection with an increased risk of heart attack and stroke. It is clear that our work is far from done."

Low immunization rates represent a national public health crisis.

People Die Needlessly

Dr. Robert Hopkins, Associate Professor at the University of Arkansas for Medical Science and a member of the Adult Immunization Advisory Board of the American College of Physicians and the organization's Arkansas Chapter Governor, detailed the terrible burden of pneumococcal disease in adults. "Up to 5,000 Americans die every year from a disease that can be prevented by vaccination," said Dr. Hopkins. "Many pneumococcal infections can be prevented or their severity significantly reduced by this simple immunization."

The decades-long increase in pertussis (whooping cough) rates was highlighted by Dr. Mark Dworkin from the Division of Epidemiology and Biostatistics at the University of Illinois at Chicago School of Public Health. According to Dr. Dworkin, "We need to use the newly available booster vaccines against pertussis for adults and adolescents widely because this may get pertussis back under control. Adults and adolescents can get coughing illness that may last for weeks or even months and they represent a large reservoir of infection putting others, such as vulnerable infants, at increased risk of infection."

Dr. Schaffner called on everyone to focus more on this important issue for the public health good. "Low immunization rates represent a national public health crisis whose consequences affect the entire country as well as affected individuals and their families. The challenges to increasing rates are real, but the benefits of achieving high vaccination rates are substantial."

11

Drug-Resistant Infectious Diseases Are a Serious Threat

Amy Gillentine

Amy Gillentine writes on health topics for the Colorado Springs Business Journal.

Antibiotic-resistant infections are one of the biggest problems facing hospitals. Overprescription of antibiotics is the major reason that so many bacteria have become resistant to the drugs. Drug resistance is costly both in terms of human life and the expense of treatment. Doctors must be careful not to prescribe antibiotics too quickly, and patients must take the drugs exactly as prescribed to combat resistance; otherwise, hospitals might be faced with infections that do not respond to any drugs.

It's the biggest threat facing health care in the United States, according to the Centers for Disease Control and Prevention [CDC]. It's a problem that increases the severity of diseases, causes longer hospital stays and drives up health care costs. "It" is antibiotic resistance. The problem has reached such a level at the nation's hospitals that the CDC, the Food and Drug Administration [FDA] and several other national health organizations have launched campaigns to increase knowledge about when to use antibiotics, and how to use them as prescribed. . . . The Colorado state Department of Public Health and Environment created Get Smart Colorado [in 2004] to address the rising problem of antibiotic resistan[t] bacteria. "We focus on the general public and health care providers," said Kelly Kast, program coordinator. "It's an increasingly serious problem. Just think what will happen if bacteria become resistant to the usual antibiotics. People go into the hospital, have to take stronger antibiotics—which have some serious side effects—and could be sicker, longer. It could get very expensive." Colorado focuses on health care providers—not just the people who take the medication. Antibiotics can be over-prescribed, Kast said. "Sometimes people come in and demand antibiotics," she said. "And doctors, wanting that customer satisfaction, will prescribe it, even if it's not necessary."

Over-prescribing antibiotics is one of the leading factors of drug-resistant bacteria.

Using Drugs as Prescribed

Use as prescribed, that's a problem, too. Some people don't take all their medication, they stop taking it when they feel better, and that can lead to resistance as well. Dr. Bruce McHaffie, a local pediatrician, said he tries to teach parents about when their children need antibiotics—and when they don't. "Sometimes they try to insist," he said. "But we just tell them that not all infections will respond to antibiotics." The health department tracks streptococcus pneumonia, the bacteria that cause common childhood ear infections. Before the 1990s, Kast said, penicillin killed the bacteria, universally. Now, the bacteria are increasingly resistant, and other drugs must be used. "And there aren't a lot of new antibiotics being created by the drug companies," Kast said. "The FDA and CDC are encouraging companies to experiment to create more, but there aren't a lot coming out right now." McHaffie said that until a few years ago, drug-resistant ear infections were an increasing problem—with 30 percent of ear infections caused by bacteria that are resistant to drugs. "But they came out with the pneumonia vaccine a few years ago," he said. "And it's less of a problem in Colorado than it was. Some places are still reporting 30 percent, 35 percent resistance." There is hope, he said. If doctors do not treat infections immediately with antibiotics, studies show that the antibiotics regain some of their effectiveness. "So if you use them only when needed, they're found to be more effective," McHaffie said. "Even with bacteria that are becoming resistant, using them (antibiotics) less frequently is a way to maintain their effectiveness."

Renewed Search for Drugs

About half the pharmaceutical companies in the United States left the antimicrobial field in the mid-1980s, according to the National Foundation for Infectious Diseases. "Recently, they are returning in response to the need," according to a white paper produced by the foundation. "Educational projects for physicians and patients should be emphasized. Antibiotic use must improve so as to preserve the efficacy of the drugs we have. More research support is needed in order to define the molecular basis for resistance and to find ways to circumvent it. Better surveillance systems for antibiotic resistance are needed. Interaction and interrelationships between surveillance groups, both in animal and human microbiology need to be established and solidified." Take antibiotics only as directed—those instructions are increasingly important, particularly during the cold and flu season, Kast said. Many people go to the doctor with sore throats, ear infections, sinus infections and colds caused by viruses, which do not respond to antibiotic treatment. "Antibiotics do not work for all infections," she said. "If you're concerned, go to the doctor. But let the doctor decide what the treatment needs to be. Overprescribing antibiotics is one of the leading factors of drug-resistant bacteria."

Drug Resistance Is Expensive

Experts agree that the cost of antibiotic resistance is substantial, but estimates range from $100 million to $30 billion annually, according to the Center for Science in the Public Interest. The National Foundation for Infectious Diseases estimates the cost to be $4 billion annually. Those resistant infections are difficult and costly to treat, according to the Center for Science in the Public Interest. For example, the cost of treating a patient with tuberculosis increases from $12,000 for a patient with a drug-susceptible strain to $180,000 for a patient with a multidrug-resistant strain. Multidrug-resistant tuberculosis (MDR-TB) is a serious public-health threat worldwide. In the United States, MDR-TB was unheard of in the 1980s. However, the number of cases of drug-resistant tuberculosis has risen precipitously since the 1990s, the association says.

Resistant tuberculosis has never been found in [Colorado's] El Paso County, said Lynn Baldvins, infection prevention program manager for Memorial Health System. But the hospital considers other drug-resistant bacteria to be a "huge problem," she said. "Methicillin-resistant staphylococcus aureus is a problem," Baldvins said. "And we take very aggressive steps. It's a concern because staphylococcus is ubiquitous, it's everywhere on our skin, in the environment. And for it to be resistant to a pretty sophisticated antibiotic, that's a concern." The cost of treating those drug-resistant infections is hard to determine, she said. "I couldn't begin to quantify it," Baldvins said. "It's hard to put a number on. The isolation costs are a big factor. It costs a lot of money to put people in isolation, and it takes longer to care for them. It takes longer for them to get well." Patients with drug-resistant bacterial infections—no matter what kind—are given special treatment at Memorial, she said. They are flagged, so when they come in for treatment, doctors know they have a drug-resistant infection. When they are hospitalized, they are put in isolation.

"The hospital also has a very aggressive hand hygiene program," she said. "Every doctor, nurse, volunteer who works with those patients must use good hand hygiene. It's how the staphylococcus spreads—poor health care hygiene. So we insist on that, all over the hospital, actually." The biggest fear: the hospital might one day see a patient who does not respond to any antibiotic treatment. "That's the worst case, that's what we're afraid of," Baldvins said. "We might have a situation where the patient has an infection, and we won't be able to eliminate that infection."

12

Hospitals Can Reduce the Threat of Infectious Disease

Institute for Healthcare Improvement

The Institute for Healthcare Improvement is a not-for-profit organization working to improve health care throughout the world by developing new ideas about patient care and helping institutions implement change.

Worldwide, methicillin-resistant Staphylococcus aureus *(MRSA), a drug-resistant strain of bacteria, is causing serious infection and death. Hospitals are instituting procedures, however, that greatly reduce the rate of infection. These procedures include effective hand hygiene, decontaminating rooms and equipment, and screening all incoming patients for MRSA colonization, even if the patients are not showing symptoms of infection. In addition, hospitals have procedures for isolating infected patients and are developing best practices for use with ventilators, catheters, and other devices. All members of the hospital staff can successfully contribute to infection reduction.*

When it comes to fighting certain serious infections, the efforts of patients and providers alike can sometimes take on heroic proportions. This is especially true when the stakes are high and the infection is not easily eradicated. Infections caused by bacteria are a case in point. They are challenging to cure because some strains have become resistant to many first-line antibiotics. Staph infections can start mildly

Institute for Healthcare Improvement, "Reducing MRSA Infections: Staying One Step Ahead," July 26, 2007. © Institute for Healthcare Improvement. Reproduced by permission.

enough—perhaps a mere boil on the skin—but can then spread quickly to produce extensive, potentially fatal skin and soft tissue infections or through the bloodstream to the lungs, bones, kidneys or heart. Staph infections are associated with substantial suffering, death, and cost.

MRSA Infections Are Lethal

The most commonly identified multidrug-resistant strain of Staph cropping up in hospitals worldwide is methicillin-resistant *Staphylococcus aureus* (MRSA). Labeled a super bug because it is resistant to so many antibiotics, MRSA is a formidable enemy: It is about two-and-a-half times more lethal than infections that are treatable with methicillin, and its incidence has increased dramatically in the past decade. ICUs [intensive care units] are the most common site of infectious outbreaks, but MRSA can show up just about anywhere in hospitals. In addition, a separate strain called community-acquired MRSA is also showing up more frequently in community settings, especially among people who live or work communally such as athletes, prisoners, children, and military personnel.

> *Hospitals that implement known best practices in combating MRSA can reduce its spread.*

According to the Centers for Disease Control and Prevention (CDC), in 1974 MRSA infections accounted for just two percent of the total number of Staph infections. Today, MRSA accounts for more than 60 percent of Staph infections. A study released in June 2007 by the Association for Professionals in Infection Control and Epidemiology (APIC) estimates that at least 5 percent of US patients—about 30,000 people—may be infected with or carrying the bug at any given time. And MRSA is by no means a challenge that only US hospitals face; numerous studies show MRSA is on the rise worldwide.

Methicillin seems to be following the path of its predecessor drug in the treatment of Staph infections: In 1950 penicillin was effective against 100 percent of Staph strains. By 1985 the miracle drug was effective against less than 5 percent of such strains. Today, MRSA is resistant not only to penicillin, but frequently to erythromycin, clindamycin, ciprofloxacin, and other quinolone antibiotics as well. Some strains have been reported to be resistant even to vancomycin (the go-to drug in the past for resistant strains) and one of the newest drugs on the market, linezolid.

The Institute for Healthcare Improvement [IHI] believes that hospitals that implement known best practices in combating MRSA can reduce its spread. Combating MRSA is a key component of IHI's 5 Million Lives Campaign, focused on reducing medical harm.

The Heavy Costs of MRSA

The human and financial toll that MRSA exacts is high. More than 126,000 hospitalized patients are infected annually, and IHI estimates that more than 5,000 patients die each year as a result. While most patients are treated successfully, particularly if the infection is identified early, hospital stays are often extended by an average 9.1 days, accounting for excess costs of about $20,000 per patient. The total cost burden to the US health care system from MRSA infections is estimated at more than $2.5 billion annually.

The epidemiology of MRSA has changed in recent years, making it increasingly tricky to detect and manage. A study published in 2002 showed that cases of community-acquired MRSA infections in children in south Texas increased fourteen-fold between 1999 and 2001. Patients with community-acquired MRSA infections are showing up in hospital emergency departments and outpatient clinics in increasing numbers. The New England Journal of Medicine published research in 2005 showing that between 8 and 20 percent of patients isolated for MRSA infections in hospitals in three major US cities acquired the infection in the community.

To further complicate matters, about two percent of the population is estimated to harbor the MRSA bacteria but, because they are healthy enough to resist infection, have no idea they are carrying something that can expose and harm others. When these "colonized" individuals enter the hospital (typically for an unrelated reason), they bring MRSA with them.

Proper hand hygiene is the single most effective means of reducing hospital-borne infections, including MRSA.

Since these patients are asymptomatic, health care professionals who care for them do not take extra precautions as they would with patients known to be infected, and inadvertently spread the bacteria to other patients who may be sicker, older, weaker, and more vulnerable to infection. In fact, the principal mode of spreading MRSA in hospitals has been found to be the contaminated hands of caregivers.

Successfully Reducing MRSA

The *5 Million Lives Campaign's How-to Guide* on reducing MRSA offers a number of steps designed to stem the spread of this infection. The *Guide* calls for caregivers to use effective hand hygiene practices; decontaminate the environment and equipment; perform active surveillance cultures; use contact precautions for infected and colonized patients; and implement device bundles [procedures for safely using intravenous lines and ventilators]. . . .

Hospitals that have systems in place to support these best practices are seeing encouraging results. For example, in a collaborative effort among the Veteran's Administration Pittsburgh Health System (VAPHS), the Pittsburgh Regional Health Initiative, both in Pittsburgh, Pennsylvania, and the CDC

[Centers for Disease Control and Prevention] a "bundle" of interventions was implemented, including standard precautions, hand hygiene, active surveillance cultures, contact precautions, and an emphasis on culture change using briefings on patient care units, leadership involvement, and other strategies. There was a 70 percent decrease in MRSA infection on one patient care unit. . . .

Effective Hand Hygiene

The importance of improving hand hygiene has finally become a priority at most US hospitals, thanks to increasing awareness that compliance with proper procedures has been historically low. Despite noteworthy examples of compliance rates now as high as 90 percent at some hospitals, experts estimate that on average US health practitioners still only comply with recommended hand hygiene procedures less than 50 percent of the time. Hand hygiene improvement advocates say this *has* to change because proper hand hygiene is the single most effective means of reducing hospital-borne infections, including MRSA.

And to drive this point home, experts say, comprehensive education is key. Guidelines call for health care professionals to clean their hands both before and after patient contact. Most caregivers don't know they should do both. Many also don't know they should clean their hands after they remove protective gloves. . . .

In addition, new products such as alcohol-based gels and foams have changed everything. "We found a big knowledge gap when we began using the alcohol hand rub," says Candace Cunningham, RN [registered nurse], MRSA Prevention Coordinator at the Veteran's Administration Pittsburgh Healthcare System. "Most people felt that washing with soap and water was superior, when the alcohol products are actually proven to be more effective." While antimicrobial soap and water are still recommended for hands that are visibly soiled or have been exposed to bodily fluids, alcohol-based gels or rubs are now preferred for routine decontamination of hands after most patient contact. These products rapidly kill bacteria and most viruses, and actually are gentler on the hands than repeated use of soap and water. . . .

Decontamination of Environment

Because MRSA survives well in a hospital environment, people can contaminate their hands by touching contaminated surfaces and objects. Patients can occasionally acquire MRSA in a room whose previous occupant was colonized or infected. Thorough and frequent cleaning of the room and equipment is a critical element in keeping MRSA at bay.

Karen Cozzens at Parkland Medical Center in New Hampshire works closely with the hospital's environmental services staff to make sure they understand their critical role in keeping patients infection-free. "They receive quite a bit of training and education on environmental precautions and hand hygiene," she says. "They are not just housekeepers, they are part of the team. I remind them and everyone else how important their role is."

Comprehensive policies and procedures, as well as checklists and evaluative tools, help the environmental services staff maintain high standards, which include twice-daily cleanings in rooms where patients are on contact precautions, with a particular focus on "high-touch" areas such as door knobs and bed rails. In addition, the bedside curtains in these isolation rooms are cleaned at discharge. Dedicated patient care equipment for colonized or infected patients, such as stethoscopes, thermometers, and blood pressure cuffs, also minimizes the opportunities to carry MRSA from room to room.

Screening for MRSA

Identifying colonized patients is a key component of reducing the spread of MRSA. While infected patients are often positively identified in the course of having their clinical specimens analyzed (for example, wound, blood, or urine samples), colonized patients are far more likely to become known through "active surveillance cultures"—routine screening of patients on admission by taking a culture from the most common reservoir site for colonized MRSA: the nose.

Culturing all admitted patients is costly and labor-intensive, but some hospitals that follow these procedures claim significantly reduced MRSA rates that pay off financially as well as clinically. Hospitals that target high-risk groups for screening focus on patients admitted from long-term care facilities, people who've been hospitalized within the past year, or those with skin wounds. Don Goldmann, MD, an infection control expert and Senior Vice President at IHI, points out that screening only high-risk groups can be effective but will miss a substantial proportion of colonized patients.

> *Patients who are colonized with MRSA . . . should be placed in a single-occupancy room to reduce the likelihood of the bacteria's spread.*

In addition, says Goldmann, nasal cultures can miss patients who are colonized on other body parts, such as the armpit, rectum, or groin. But whatever surveillance strategy a hospital chooses, says Goldmann, "knowledge is power."

"Active surveillance cultures are the best way to document the extent of the problem on a particular unit or in the hospital as a whole, while culturing the patients again at the time of discharge can help assess the success of the hospital's infection control effort," says Goldmann. An effective program, he says, incorporates reliable hand hygiene, contact precautions, and environmental cleaning and disinfection, as well as excellent compliance with central venous catheter and ventilator care. "It's the combination of these steps, performed reliably, that can rapidly reduce the percentage of patients who acquire MRSA while they are in the hospital.". . .

Isolating Infected Patients

Patients who are colonized with MRSA, and particularly those who are actually infected, should be placed in a single-occupancy room to reduce the likelihood of the bacteria's spread. Caregivers should rigorously practice effective hand hygiene, don gloves and gowns when they enter the room, and discard them upon leaving.

When hospitals lack sufficient private rooms, MRSA-colonized patients can be placed in semi-private rooms and contact precautions must be strictly observed. Here again, says IHI's Fran Griffin, visual cues can help. "One hospital uses red tape on the floor around the area of the patient's bed," she says. "Staff know that they must use contact precautions if they cross the red line. It's not based on whether or not they even touch the patient," At Parkland Medical Center in New Hampshire, Infection Control Director Karen Cozzens says all patients on contact precautions get a special green isolation wristband, so that anyone who comes into contact with the patient knows to be especially vigilant.

The challenge here is one of timing: It can take 48 hours or longer to grow a MRSA culture. Some hospitals opt to pre-emptively place all newly admitted patients on contact precautions pending the outcome of their screening test, but this can be costly both in terms of supplies and extra staff time. Others use gloves for all contact with patients until the results of the screening are back. In either scenario, says IHI's Fran Griffin, "the key is to make sure you have systems in place to get real-time notification about MRSA-positive patients to the front-line staff as quickly as possible."

Still other hospitals are opting for a newer technology that provides results of MRSA testing within a few hours. Called polymerase chain reaction (PCR) assay, it requires a significant investment in new lab technology, but Dr. Jeremias Murillo at Newark Beth Israel Hospital says it pays for itself in the savings from fewer MRSA infections. "A lot of hospitals struggle with this," he says. "They can't get the new machine because it's too expensive. But in our NICU [neonatal intensive care unit], we've probably saved $500,000 in one year by reducing our infection rate so dramatically." And it means that babies get treatment more quickly, and don't have to be in isolation a moment longer than necessary.

Best Practices

Patients with invasive devices such as central venous catheters and ventilators are at greater risk for developing hospital-acquired infections, both because of the invasive devices, and the severity of their underlying illnesses. For these patients who may be colonized with MRSA, the risk is increased and extreme care must be taken to prevent infection.

Hospitals that have been successful at beating back MRSA share a common culture that emphasizes teamwork and the possibility of excellence.

As part of it's 100,000 Lives Campaign and now the 5 Million Lives Campaign, IHI developed and disseminated information about the implementation of "bundles"—groupings of best practices that individually improve care, but when applied together result in substantially greater improvement. . . .

Chris Farmer says the system's cross-infection matrix allows staff to "get out ahead" of an epidemic by tracking who MRSA patients have been in contact with during their hospital stay. "The tracking system has helped us enormously. Within minutes we know who might have been exposed and where they are for rapid screening and isolation purposes. We've gone from fighting fires and chasing paperwork to getting computers to do the administrative workload, so the infection control staff can do what they should be doing,"

A Group Effort

Hospitals that have been successful at beating back MRSA share a common culture that emphasizes teamwork and the possibility of excellence. "We talk about getting to zero," says Chris Farmer in Australia. "Some people can't believe we can do it, but we've seen it. We've achieved perfection for periods of time, and now the challenge is staying there."

The cultural transformation at the VA in Pittsburgh became evident to Jon Lloyd when he attended a staff meeting about preventing MRSA that included more than 100 health care workers from all specialties and vocations. "At our first meeting, we asked the staff who was responsible for infection control. Most people pointed to our Infection Control people. A year later, we posed the same question to a similar group. Almost every hand in the room went up."

13

Climate Change Increases the Threat of Infectious Diseases

Amy Greer, Victoria Ng, and David Fisman

Amy Greer, Victoria Ng, and David Fisman are researchers with the Research Institute of the Hospital for Sick Children in Toronto, Canada.

Climate, environment, and infectious disease share a close relationship. It is likely that climate change caused by greenhouse gases will lead to an increase of all kinds of diseases, including animal-, insect-, water-, and food-borne diseases. The areas where these diseases occur will also expand. Migrations from flood and drought areas will increase disease transmissions as people who have not traditionally lived near each other will be in closer proximity. Finally, the warming Arctic may cause an increase in illness for the indigenous population in the form of contaminated seafood and botulism.

Human activities have caused a sharp increase in greenhouse gases, including carbon dioxide, nitrous oxide and methane, in the atmosphere, which has led to unprecedented changes in the earth's climate. The Intergovernmental Panel on Climate Change was established by the United Nations Environment Program and the World Meteorological Organization in 1988 to provide objective analysis of data related to climate change. The panel comprises scientists from around the globe and aims to present the scientific, technical and socioeconomic issues arising from the data to government decision-makers in a policy-neutral context.

Amy Greer, Victoria Ng, and David Fisman, "Climate Change and Infectious Diseases in North America," *CMAJ*, vol. 178, March 11, 2008, pp. 715–22. Copyright © 2008 Canadian Medical Association. Reproduced by permission.

In April 2007, the panel issued a report on the impact of global climate change on human and animal populations. This report was based on about 30,000 observations of changes in physical and biological systems worldwide. More than 90% of these changes are attributable to human activities such as the combustion of fossil fuels. The panel's fourth assessment report includes projections for regions including North America. These projections include warmer temperatures, more rainfall because of an increased fraction of precipitation falling as rain rather than snow, and more frequent droughts, wildfires and extreme weather events such as hurricanes and tornados. Warming is predicted to be most severe in the northernmost latitudes.

> *Climate changes . . . are likely to influence the burden and incidence of infectious diseases in more developed regions, including North America.*

Some of the health effects attributable to climate change are directly related to changing environmental conditions. The Public Health Agency of Canada anticipates increased burden of disease as a result of thermal stress and more frequent extreme weather events, and some projected direct effects of climate change on human health, such as heat-related morbidity and injuries, have been previously reviewed. However, climate and weather patterns are important physical components of complex ecosystems and any major change in the nonliving component of an ecosystem will affect living components, including microbes, insect vectors, animal reservoirs and susceptible humans, and change the incidence and distribution of infectious diseases.

Increasing Infectious Disease

The close relation between climate, environment and infectious disease in the developing world are well recognized. For example, the importance of rainfall and drought in the occurrence of malaria, the influence of the dry season on epidemic meningococcal disease in the sub-Saharan African "meningitis belt" and the importance of warm ocean waters in driving cholera occurrence in the Ganges River delta and elsewhere in Asia are well described. Indeed, there is widespread concern about the potential impact of global climate change on the distribution and burden of these and other infectious threats in the developing world.

Warmer winter temperatures may facilitate the establishment of imported mosquito-borne diseases in countries from which they have historically been absent.

The relation between ecosystems, infectious diseases and global climate change are less intuitive in the context of more developed countries where clean drinking water, reduced exposure to insect vectors, higher-quality housing and other advantages partly mitigate such threats. However, climate changes projected to occur in the coming decades are likely to influence the burden and incidence of infectious diseases in more developed regions, including North America. . . .

Disease Range Will Expand

Climate change may affect zoonoses (infectious diseases of animal origin that may be transmitted to humans) in 3 ways: it may increase the range or abundance of animal reservoirs or insect vectors, prolong transmission cycles, or increase the importation of vectors [intermediate disease transmitters such as ticks and mosquitoes] or animal reservoirs (e.g., by boat or air) to new regions, which may cause the establishment of diseases in those regions. For example, the burden of Lyme disease (a tick-borne borreliosis) is likely to change substantially in North America and Europe. Currently, endemic Lyme disease is uncommon in Canada, and established populations of competent vectors (vectors that are capable of allowing the pathogen to complete its lifecycle, such as *Ixodes scapularis* and *Ixodes pacificus* [species of ticks]) are limited largely to southern Ontario, Nova Scotia and British Columbia. However, temperature determines the northernmost extent of tick populations. Mathematical models suggest that tick abundance may greatly increase in southern Canada, with a northern expansion of about 200 km [kilometers] by the year 2020. This rate of expansion would be sufficient to establish vector populations in Alberta and Saskatchewan. . . .

Early Spring Means More Disease

The transmission of vector-borne zoonoses may also be enhanced by earlier onset of spring, resulting in a prolonged amplification cycle. West Nile virus, which appeared in Canada in 2002, has an amplification cycle that involves mosquitoes and birds. Human infections become more likely as the proportion of "bridge" vectors (mosquitoes that bite both birds and humans) increases: In temperate regions, virus amplification begins with the onset of mosquito activity in spring. Human risk peaks in late summer or early autumn, and risk decreases with the disappearance of mosquitoes in autumn. An earlier onset of spring would prolong the amplification cycle resulting in an increased incidence of human infection. The impact of increased precipitation on mosquito ecosystems is complicated. Transmission risk could increase because of increased mosquito breeding sites. Alternatively, increased numbers of mosquito predators and decreased geographic concentrations of amplifying hosts (i.e., birds) attributable to a rise in the distribution of water sources may lower the risk of transmission.

Whether climate change will facilitate re-establishment of autochthonous (locally acquired) malaria in the United States and Canada, where it was once endemic, is unclear. However, prolonged amplification cycles and warmer winter temperatures may facilitate the establishment of imported mosquito-borne diseases in countries from which they have historically been absent. For example, in 2007 chikungunya fever, a mosquito-borne disease endemic in parts of Africa and Asia, caused a large outbreak of disease in northeastern Italy, presumably following importation of infected mosquitoes via boat or air. The onset of winter weather likely contributed to the control of this outbreak, but warming trends may make the control of future importation-related outbreaks more difficult.

Climate change may . . . increase the risk of plague in western states and provinces.

Travel and Disease

Residents or temperate regions of North America may also be affected by increased incidence and distribution of vector-borne diseases in other countries because of high rates of travel to subtropical and tropical countries. For example, it is estimated that Canadians took over 2 million trips to Mexico, Cuba and the Dominican Republic in 2006 alone. As dengue and malaria activity are projected to increase in Latin America, the Caribbean, Asia and Africa, an increase in travel-related dengue fever and malaria in returning travellers is likely. Marked discrepancies in dengue incidence in contiguous geographical areas (e.g., along the US—Mexican border) suggest that both vector abundance and economic factors, such as the availability of air conditioning, contribute to disease risk. Travellers who use more luxurious accommodations and insect repellents that contain diethyltoluamide (DEET) may be relatively protected. Nonetheless, the impact of such increases on local populations, combined with emerging resistance to antimalarial agents and the recent resurgence of malaria in a number of urban areas in Jamaica and India, are cause for substantial concern both for travel medicine practitioners and for those concerned about global health.

Rodents and Disease

Climate change is also likely to impact the distribution and burden of zoonotic diseases that are not dependent on insect vectors for transmission. Pathogens such as the Sin Nombre virus, a cause of hantavirus pulmonary syndrome, are harboured by rodent species that are especially abundant in the southwestern United States and in western states and provinces. Rodent population density appears to be a key driver of disease in humans, who are often infected after exposure to dust contaminated by rodent urine (e.g., while sweeping out storage spaces). Recent surges in hantavirus infection have been attributed to the El Niño-type weather conditions, which may become predominant with future climate change, suggesting that hantavirus pulmonary syndrome incidence may increase in coming decades. Climate change may similarly increase the risk of plague in western states and provinces.

Water- and Food-Borne Diseases

Water- and food-borne diseases are a major cause of mortality worldwide and an important cause of morbidity in developed countries. Water-borne pathogens include viral, bacterial and protozoan agents of gastroenteritis and pneumonic pathogens such as *Legionella* species. Many of these pathogens (e.g., verotoxigenic *Escherichia coli, Campylobacter* species and viral pathogens) are also important causes of food-borne illness, as are bacterial pathogens such as *Salmonella and Shigella* species.

Water-borne diseases occur despite state-of-the-art water treatment technology. For example, a 1989 cryptosporidiosis outbreak tied to a municipal water supply in Milwaukee, Wisconsin, affected an estimated 400,000 people. The Walkerton, Ontario, disaster in 2,000 underscored the vulnerability of populations to water-borne disease [2500 people sickened and at least seven died as a result of *E. coli* contamination of the town's water supply]. The incidence of both water- and food-borne diseases is expected to increase as a result of climate change. Large water-borne disease outbreaks have been linked to extreme precipitation events, which are expected to increase in frequency in coming decades. In addition, most cases of water- and food-borne gastroenteritis, particularly illness related to *Campylobacter* and *Salmonella*, exhibit a distinct summertime pattern of occurrence. Although it is possible that seasonality is due to behavioural patterns (e.g., barbecuing or swimming in the summer), the association between warmer temperatures and disease suggests that rates of water- and food-borne illness are likely to increase with rising temperatures.

The incidence of pneumonic infections due to water-borne infectious agents, such as legionellosis (Legionnaire disease) and melioidosis, is also likely to be affected by climate change. Legionellosis incidence peaks during warmer months and risk appears to increase with rainy, humid weather. Melioidosis is an infectious disease caused by the bacterium *Burkholderia pseudomallei* and is endemic in southeast Asia and Australia. Cyclones appear to be associated with increased risk of severe melioidosis, perhaps because of aerosolization of the bacterium by stormy weather.

Globally, the water-borne enteric disease most likely to increase in the face of global climate change is cholera, a diarrheal disease with a high case-fatality rate caused by infection with toxigenic strains of *Vibrio cholerae*, which remains an important cause or death in the developing world. Risk increases with warmer water temperatures, suggesting that global cholera activity may increase sharply in the face of climate change. Such increases pose a risk not only to developing countries, but also to developed countries via importation of disease. Nontoxigenic strains of *V. cholerae* and other noncholera *Vibrio* (e.g., *Vibrio parahemolyticus* and *Vibrio vulnificus*) may also become more frequent agents of disease as a result of increasing ocean temperatures and increasing frequency of extreme weather events. For example, cases of illness due to these micro-organisms occurred in association with Hurricane Katrina in 2005.

The burden of parasitic diseases in the North may increase with warming.

Seasonality and Migration

Many respiratory pathogens, including influenza, respiratory syncytial virus and *Streptococcus pneumoniae*, exhibit winter seasonality that is often attributed to seasonal changes in temperature or population behaviour (e.g., indoor crowding). In fact, these phenomena are poorly understood and causal mechanisms are difficult to establish owing to seasonal coincidence of multiple exposures. If cold temperatures are an important driver of respiratory disease, climate change might be expected to attenuate the impact of influenza epidemics. Data based on influenza activity during the El Niño Seasonal Oscillation (an intermittent inversion of Pacific Ocean thermal gradients) suggest that this may be the case. El Niño is associated with changes in weather patterns similar to those projected to occur in coming decades. In this sense, study of disease trends in the presence and absence of El Niño may provide insight into future disease patterns.

Climate change also has the potential to indirectly affect communicable disease transmission. The forced migration of people because of drought or flooding could increase the transmission of many communicable diseases because of enhanced intermingling of populations that have previously been isolated from one another. Large-scale migrations have been associated with surges in communicable diseases and emergence of novel infections throughout recorded history. Forced migration may ultimately be a more important driver of changes in infectious disease epidemiology than other effects. . . .

Arctic Warming

Arctic regions are uniquely vulnerable ecosystems that have experienced warming trends that are more substantial than those experienced elsewhere in North America. An increased incidence of water- and food-borne disease and zoonoses appears inevitable. The economic, social and environmental impact of disease emergence in Arctic regions will place a heavy burden on already underserved communities. Hunting and traditional means of food preparation may also increase the probability of contracting an infectious disease.

Increases in ocean temperatures have been linked to outbreaks of gastroenteritis as a result of infection by noncholera *Vibrio* species, which may have been acquired through consumption of contaminated seafood. Likewise, the risk of botulism from consumption of traditional fermented meats is enhanced by increased ambient air temperatures.

Changing ecosystems also disrupt the ecology of wildlife populations in ways that are likely to increase the risk of zoonotic disease. Climate-driven increases in rabbit and predator populations (e.g., fox) may augment the risk of tularemia and rabies. Warmer temperatures and longer summers increase the number of amplification cycles for parasites of food animals (e.g., *Trichinella* and *Echinococcus* species) and lead to longer summer hunting seasons. These parasites cause diseases that are largely concentrated in northern communities, and the burden of parasitic diseases in the North may increase with warming.

14

Public Health Systems Are Ready for Diseases Caused by Climate Change

Julie L. Gerberding

From 2002 until 2009, Julie L. Gerberding has been the director of the Centers for Disease Control and Prevention (CDC), a division of the U.S. Department of Health and Human Services, headquartered in Atlanta, Georgia.

The Centers for Disease Control and Prevention (CDC) is leading the effort to prepare for the health consequences of climate change. The CDC has demonstrated expertise in several key areas, including tracking the health impact of environmental hazards; following water-borne, food-borne, vector-borne and animal-carried diseases; and preparedness planning. In addition, the CDC has a strong infrastructure that provides expert communication regarding diseases to the public. The CDC is also a leader in health protection research. Therefore, many of the CDC's existing programs will provide the groundwork necessary to deal with the disease potential of climate change.

The health of all individuals is influenced by the health of people, animals, and the environment around us. Many trends within this larger, interdependent ecologic system influence public health on a global scale, including climate change.

Julie L. Gerberding, "Testimony on Climate Change and Public Health," Senate Committee on Environment and Public Works, United States Senate, October 23, 2007. Reproduced by permission.

The public health response to such trends requires a holistic understanding of disease and the various external factors influencing public health. It is within this larger context where the greatest challenges and opportunities for protecting and promoting public health occur.

Preparing for Climate Change

Climate change is anticipated to have a broad range of impacts on the health of Americans and the nation's public health infrastructure. As the nation's public health agency, CDC is uniquely poised to lead efforts to anticipate and respond to the health effects of climate change. Preparedness for the health consequences of climate change aligns with traditional public health contributions, and—like preparedness for terrorism and pandemic influenza—reinforces the importance of a strong public health infrastructure. CDC's expertise and programs in the following areas provide the strong platform needed:

Public Health Tracking: CDC has a long history of tracking occurrence and trends in diseases and health outcomes. CDC is pioneering new ways to understand the impacts of environmental hazards on people's health. For example, CDC's Environmental Public Health Tracking Program has funded several states to build a health surveillance system that integrates environmental exposures and human health outcomes. This system, the Tracking Network, [went] live in 2008, providing information on how health is affected by environmental hazards. The Tracking Network will contain critical data on the incidence, trends, and potential outbreaks of disease, including those affected by climate change.

Surveillance of Water-borne, Food-borne, Vector-borne, and Zoonotic Diseases: CDC also has a long history of surveillance of infectious, zoonotic [diseases carried by animals], and vector-borne [carried by an intermediary host, such as mosquitoes] diseases. Preparing for climate change will involve working closely with state and local partners to document whether potential changes in climate have an impact on infectious and other diseases and to use this information to help protect Americans from the potential change in a variety of dangerous water-borne, food-borne, vector-borne, and zoonotic diseases. CDC has developed ArboNet, the national arthropod-borne viral disease tracking system. Currently, this system supports the nationwide West Nile virus surveillance system that links all 50 states and four large metropolitan areas to a central database that records and maps cases in humans and animals and would detect changes in real-time in the distribution and prevalence of cases of arthropod-borne viral diseases. CDC also supports the major food-borne surveillance and investigative networks of FoodNet and PulseNet, which rapidly identify and provide detailed data on cases of food-borne illnesses, on the organisms that cause them, and on the foods that are the sources of infection. Altered weather patterns resulting from climate change may affect the distribution and incidence of food- and water-borne diseases, and these changes can be identified and tracked through PulseNet.

Just as we prepare for terrorism and pandemic influenza, we should use these principles and prepare for health impacts from climate change.

Geographic Information System (GIS): At the CDC, GIS technology has been applied in unique and powerful ways to a variety or public health issues. It has been used in data collection, mapping, and communication to respond to issues as wide-ranging and varied as the World Trade Center collapse, avian flu, SARS [severe acute respiratory syndrome], and Rift Valley fever. In addition, GIS technology was used to map issues of importance during the CDC response to Hurricane Katrina. This technology represents an additional tool for the public health response to climate change.

Modeling: Model projections of future climate change can be used as inputs into models that assess the impact of climate change on public health. CDC has conducted heat stroke modeling for the city of Philadelphia to predict the most vulnerable populations at risk for hyperthermia. In light of these projections, CDC has initiated efforts to model the impact of heat waves on urban populations to identify those people most vulnerable to hyperthermia.

Preparedness Planning: Just as we prepare for terrorism and pandemic influenza, we should use these principles and prepare for health impacts from climate change. For example, to respond to the multiple threats posed by heat waves, the urban environment, and climate change, CDC scientists have focused prevention efforts on developing tools that local emergency planners and decision-makers can use to prepare for and respond to heat waves. In collaboration with other Federal partners, CDC participated in the development of an *Excessive Heat Events Guidebook,* which provides a comprehensive set of guiding principles and a menu of options for cities and localities to use in the development of Heat Response Plans. These plans clearly define specific roles and responsibilities of government and non-governmental organizations during heat waves. They identify local populations at increased high risk for heat-related illness and death and determine which strategies will be used to reach them during heat emergencies.

Training and Education of Public Health Professionals: Preparing for the health consequences of climate change requires that professionals have the skills required to conceptualize the impending threats, integrate a wide variety of public health and other data in surveillance activities, work closely with other agencies and sectors, and provide effective health communication for vulnerable populations regarding the evolving threat of climate change. CDC is holding a series of five workshops to further explore key dimensions of climate change and public health, including drinking water, heat waves, health communication, vector-borne illness, and vulnerable populations.

Health Protection Research: CDC can promote research to further elucidate the specific relationships between climate change and various health outcomes, including predictive models and evaluations of interventions. Research efforts can also identify the magnitude of health effects and populations at greatest risk. For example, CDC has conducted research on the relationship between hantavirus pulmonary syndrome and rainfall, as well as research assessing the impact of climate variability and climate change on temperature-related morbidity and mortality. This information will help enable public health action to be targeted and will help determine the best methods of communicating risk. CDC can serve as a credible source of information on health risks and actions that individuals can take to reduce their risk. In addition, CDC has several state-of-the-art laboratories conducting research on such issues as chemicals and human exposure, radiological testing, and infectious diseases. This research capacity is an asset in working to more fully understand the health consequences of climate change.

Many of the activities needed to protect Americans from adverse health effects of climate change are mutually beneficial for overall public health.

Communication: CDC has expertise in communicating to the general public health and risk information, and has deployed this expertise in areas as diverse as smoking, HIV infection, and cancer screening. Effective communication can alert the public to health risks associated with climate change, and encourage constructive protective behaviors.

Preparing at the Local Level

While CDC can offer technical support and expertise in these and other activities, much of this work needs to be carried out at the state and local level. For example, CDC can support climate change preparedness activities in public health agencies, and climate change and health research in universities, as is currently practiced for a variety of other health challenges.

An effective public health response to climate change can prevent injuries, illnesses, and death and enhance overall public health preparedness. Protecting Americans from adverse health effects of climate change directly correlates to CDC's four overarching Health Protection Goals of Healthy People in Every Stage of Life, Healthy People in Healthy Places, People Prepared for Emerging Health Threats, and Healthy People in a Healthy World.

While we still need more focus and emphasis on public health preparedness for climate change, many of our existing programs and scientific expertise provide a solid foundation to move forward. Many of the activities needed to protect Americans from adverse health effects of climate change are mutually beneficial for overall public health. In addition, health and the environment are closely linked. Because of this linkage it is also important that potential health effects of environmental solutions be fully considered.

15

Public Health Systems Are Not Prepared for the Challenges of Climate Change

John Balbus et al.

John Balbus is the health program director and chief health scientist of the Environmental Defense Fund.

Climate change will cause unprecedented public health risks, including increases in infectious diseases caused by warmer temperatures. Poor people and regions will be most affected by the changes. Because the public health systems in the United States are not centralized and the government does not fund them adequately, the necessary planning for the health risks of climate change has not taken place adequately. In addition, most emergency medical facilities are not adequately prepared to cope with the health impacts of climate change. Although the United States has the resources to deal with the impacts, it has shown a lack of planning and implementation of protective measures.

Global climate change currently contributes to disease and premature death worldwide, increasing the risk of adverse health impacts from more severe heatwaves and other extreme weather events, reduced air quality, malnutrition and infectious diseases. Even if immediate, drastic cuts in greenhouse gas emissions are implemented, the planet is committed to additional significant changes in climate because of processes already set in motion by human activities in the last

John Balbus et al., "Introduction," *Are We Ready? Preparing for the Public Health Challenges of Climate Change*, 2008. Reproduced by permission.

century. Recent assessments conclude that this climate change to which we are already committed could increase the incidence of illness and mortality in the United States. Climate-related diseases and disasters that occur outside of the country may also threaten U.S. public health, as travelers and refugees import novel diseases. The unprecedented nature of climate change is likely to result in the emergence of unexpected risks to public health, as well.

Coping with Climate Change

Given the challenge that U.S. public health faces, the agencies and organizations that are responsible for protecting public health need to increase their capacity to cope with climate change–related health risks. Increased public health preparedness would reduce the severity and extent of climate-related heath impacts. Effective heatwave early warning systems in the United States, for example, have been shown to reduce the number of deaths during a heatwave, suggesting that improving awareness of the risks of extreme heat would prevent future mortality. Surveillance programs could also expand to include monitoring for the spread of vectorborne and zoonotic [animal-borne] diseases to areas where the temperatures are currently too cold to support the organisms that participate in disease-spreading cycles. Regulations can take into consideration more ozone formation and faster growth of pathogens with warmer temperatures. Engagement of the public health community should also include evaluating the health implications of major climate change and using public health expertise in behavior change to aid measures for reducing greenhouse gas emissions.

Despite the evidence of increasing climate change, and thus the importance of proactive development and deployment of public health interventions, it is unclear to what extent public health professionals in general view climate change as a public health issue. Although many of the anticipated health threats of climate change are within the current focus areas of public health departments, public health professionals may not be associating these problems with climate change, and hence may not be adequately preparing for future needs. . . .

The United States is experiencing long-term changes in temperature, precipitation and intensity of extreme weather events that are consistent with global climate change. These changes may affect the geographic range, incidence and severity of health outcomes that are sensitive to weather and climate, and they are likely to have dramatic impacts on human health and well-being. A host of important factors, including baseline health and nutritional status of the population, financial resources, access to medical, care and effectiveness of public health programs will also moderate the ultimate severity of these health outcomes.

Likely Impacts of Climate Change

A recent assessment of the potential human health impacts of climate change, conducted for the U.S. Climate Change Science Program, concluded that climate change poses a risk for U.S. populations. Official assessments consistently state that the following impacts are likely.

- Increased frequency, intensity and length of heatwaves, leading to increased mortality, particularly in regions currently vulnerable to heatwaves;

- Increased frequency and intensity, of floods, droughts, windstorms and wildfire, resulting in increases in adverse health outcomes, including mental health impacts associated with these events;

- Increased exposures to ground-level ozone and aeroallergens, thereby exacerbating cardiovascular and pulmonary illness;

- Shift of the temperature distribution towards warmer temperatures, leading to increased risk of several food- and waterborne diseases. . . .

Climate change will likely magnify health disparities as more frequent and severe heatwaves, hurricanes, wildfires and floods cause deaths and injury while simultaneously damaging health infrastructure.

Changes in vectorborne and zoonotic diseases are more uncertain; such diseases currently tracked in the United States are unlikely to pose a significant threat as long as current levels of public health programs are maintained.

Even assuming that the capacity of the United States to implement effective and timely adaptation measures remains high, the possibility of severe climate-related health impacts is not eliminated. The nature of climate-related risks, such as those posed by extreme weather events and conditions, means that some adverse health outcomes are unlikely to be avoidable, even with efforts to improve population resilience. For this reason, members of the public health community recognize that reducing greenhouse gas emissions and enhancing the effectiveness of the public health system are absolutely essential to protect people and prevent climate-related illness and death.

Vulnerable Groups

Severe health impacts will not be evenly distributed across populations and regions, but will be concentrated in the most vulnerable groups and regions. Particularly vulnerable populations include children, older adults, pregnant women and those with pre-existing medical conditions or mobility and cognitive constraints. Poverty also increases susceptibility to climate-related health effects independently of any associations with medical conditions conferring risk. Hurricane Katrina [2005] demonstrated that climate-related health impacts can place a disproportionate burden on disadvantaged populations. During extreme weather events, poor people and communities may lack adequate shelter or access to protective resources such as air conditioning, transportation, health care and emergency assistance. Climate change will likely magnify health disparities as more frequent and severe heatwaves, hurricanes, wildfires and floods cause deaths and injury while simultaneously damaging health infrastructure.

In addition, climate change poses greater health risks for people living in regions that have marginal water supplies, are low lying and prone to flooding or coastal surges, or experience more severe ecosystem changes as a response to changing climate (such as residents in the permafrost areas of the Arctic). Dense urban areas characterized by lack of vegetation and high proportions of paved surfaces are also likely to experience greater heat stress. Public health departments can use an understanding of local and regional ecosystems and built environment characteristics to help identify the most vulnerable populations and target interventions specifically for them.

Overburdened and Underfunded

The U.S. public health system is a network of organizations, people and information and communication systems dedicated to protecting and promoting health and preventing disease. With no single entity in charge, responsibility is divided among federal, state and local agencies, which differ greatly in resources, services, staffing and performance capacity. In general, public health constitutes a small share of the nation's overall health expenditures. Although state and local public health agencies run programs ranging from disease surveillance to Medicaid administration, their spending made up less than 2.32% of all U.S. health spending in 2005, down from 2.37% in 2004. The Institute of Medicine has concluded that the public health infrastructure is "neglected," with serious deficits in workforce, information systems and organizational capacity.

In the aftermath of the 2001 terrorist attacks, substantial increases in federal funding for preparedness and response to public health emergencies have allowed state and local health departments to significantly improve their emergency response capacities for bioterrorist attacks and pandemic influenza. The Public Health Emergency Preparedness Cooperative has provided more than $5 billion to state, local, tribal and territorial public health departments since 2002, which has supported reporting networks and public health professional training, as well as the development of the Strategic National Stockpile and Cities Readiness Initiative.

However, integrating preparedness activities with other public health responsibilities has been challenging. Although emergency preparedness funding has been distributed, local, state and federal public health agencies are only at the rudimentary stages of planning, sorting out responsibilities, sharing resources and establishing robust communication networks. And even as state and local health agencies work to meet preparedness goals, funding has declined. Since 2005, a more than 25% decline in public health preparedness funding threatens the sustainability of new emergency preparedness programs.

The increasing burden of chronic and emerging diseases has also added new responsibilities to already overburdened public health systems, but per capita spending and workforce availability have not kept pace. Public health remains seriously underfunded. . . .

Public Health Response

Responses to Hurricanes Katrina and Rita raise strong concerns as to how well public health systems will respond to increasingly frequent, severe and prolonged disasters because of climate change. While there were some short-term success stories with these hurricanes, such as the limitation in food- and waterborne infectious disease outbreaks, there were serious shortcomings in the continuity of health services, follow-up of vulnerable populations and protective environmental health controls. In response, several federal programs are aiming to improve coordination by targeting limited resources and supplying accurate information to health care providers after climate-related disasters and disease outbreaks. Nonetheless, public confidence is low. In 2007, nearly 60% of Americans felt that their community would be unprepared to respond to a natural disaster. A 2006 White House report on lessons learned from Hurricane Katrina determined that nationwide disaster preparedness will "require significant and lasting change to the status quo, to include adjustments to policy, structure, and mindset."

[The] public health effects of climate change remain largely unaddressed.

Current disease surveillance and response capabilities are likely insufficient to effectively address novel climate-related health effects. Augmenting various CDC tracking and monitoring systems, including ArboNET, FoodNet and PulseNet, could help combat potential mosquito- and foodborne disease increases caused by climate change. Twelve states presently lack an electronic disease surveillance system compatible with the national system, and nationwide disease monitoring remains disconnected from monitoring of related health, behavioral and environmental factors. A similar gap exists between human and animal health agencies, which if bridged, would facilitate quicker responses to climate-related emerging zoonotic disease outbreaks. In addition, public health departments and state public health laboratories have reported difficulty recruiting and retaining qualified epidemiologists and laboratory scientists.

Medical Facilities Poorly Prepared

Emergency medical facilities are a critical element of preparedness for climate change, especially for projected increases in extreme weather events. A series of recent Institute of Medicine reports raised concerns that the nation's facilities are challenged by day-to-day patient loads and are poorly prepared to deal with large disasters.

Research on the health impacts of climate change is also essential for anticipating and reducing health risks. A 2007 Congressional Research Service report on federal climate change expenditures calls research "the cornerstone of the U.S. strategy to address global climate change." However, funding for research on the health impacts of climate change is minimal. Between FY [fiscal year] 2003 and 2007, funding for health research constituted less than 5% of the overall U.S. Climate Change Science Program (CCSP) budget. And of the $50 million dollars spent on CCSP research in the Department of Health and Human Services, the vast majority went to research on the effects of UV [ultraviolet] radiation and the effectiveness of sunblocks, rather than health issues more directly related to climate change. A National Academy of Sciences review of the CCSP noted the lack of progress in understanding human impacts and vulnerabilities, citing the low level of funding and "atomized" research effects among multiple agencies.

A nationwide climate change health sector assessment updated in 2006 noted that although the United States has a high capacity to respond to climate change, little implementation of adaptive measures has been documented. The Director of the Division of Environmental Hazards and Health Effects at the CDC asserted in March 2007 that the "public health effects of climate change remain largely unaddressed."

Organizations to Contact

The editors have compiled the following list of organizations concerned with the issues debated in this book. The descriptions are derived from materials provided by the organizations. All have publications or information available for interested readers. The list was compiled on the date of publication of the present volume; the information provided here may change. Be aware that many organizations take several weeks or longer to respond to inquiries, so allow as much time as possible.

The Carter Center
One Copenhill, Atlanta, GA   30307
(404) 420-5100
e-mail: carterweb@emory.edu
Web site: www.cartercenter.org

Founded by former president Jimmy and First Lady Rosalynn Carter, the Carter Center is a nonprofit organization dedicated to "creating a world in which every man, woman, and child has the opportunity to enjoy good health and live in peace." The Web site includes information regarding the Carter Center's work in preventing disease in Latin America and Africa. The site also provides videos, brochures, and articles.

**The Center for Infectious Disease Research
and Policy (CIDRAP)**
University of Minnesota, Minneapolis, MN   55455
(612) 626-6770
e-mail: cidrap@umn.edu
Web site: www.cidrap.umn.edu

The Center for Infectious Disease Research and Policy addresses public health preparedness and emerging infectious disease response. Some of the center's main work focuses on pandemic influenza preparedness, bioterrorism response, and information gathering and dissemination. The Web site offers sections on influenza, bioterrorism, biosecurity, food safety, and other topics such as SARS, West Nile virus, and monkey pox, complete with many articles, facts, and resources.

The Centers for Disease Control and Prevention (CDC)
1600 Clifton Rd., Atlanta, GA   30333
(800) 232-4636
e-mail: cdcinfo@cdc.gov
Web site: www.cdc.gov

A division of the U.S. Department of Health and Human Services, the CDC is the nation's premier public health organization. The mission of the CDC is "to promote health and quality of life by preventing and controlling disease, injury, and disability." The CDC Web site provides a wealth of useful and understandable materials on the subject of infectious diseases, including fact sheets, publications, news articles, and statistics.

Committee to Reduce Infection Deaths (RID)
Attn. Betsy McCaughey, New York, NY   10028
(212) 369-3329
Web site: www.hospitalinfection.org

RID is a nonprofit educational campaign and advocacy group devoted to fighting the causes of hospital infections. Its Web site includes information about MRSA, the state of hygiene in American hospitals, and a list of fifteen steps patients can take to reduce their risk for hospital-originated infections. Also listed on the site are links to other publications, a newsletter, and a blog. Educational materials can be ordered through the RID Web site.

Global Solutions for Infectious Diseases (GSID)
830 Dubuque Ave., South San Francisco, CA   94080
(650) 228-7901
Web site: www.gsid.org

Global Solutions for Infectious Diseases is a nonprofit organization dedicated to the expansion of low-cost diagnostic tools and prevention of infectious diseases in less-developed countries. The group is targeting HIV/AIDS and is working to develop a vaccine for the disease. The GSID Web site has many helpful articles as well as descriptions of GSID worldwide projects.

Infectious Disease Research Institute (IDRI)
1124 Columbia St., Ste. 400, Seattle, Washington   98104
(206) 381-0883
e-mail: office@idri.org
Web site: www.idri.org

The Infectious Disease Research Institute is a nonprofit biotech research organization that states that its mission is to "target diseases that largely affect individuals living in economically challenged countries that have difficulty meeting the public health burden of disease." IDRI's goal is to find cures and preventative measures to combat these diseases. The IDRI Web site includes an informative newsletter as well as specific information on diseases such as tuberculosis, malaria, and leprosy, among others.

Malaria Consortium
Head Office Development House, London   EC2A 4LT
   United Kingdom
+44 (0)20 7549 0210
e-mail: info@malariaconsortium.org
Web site: www.malariaconsortium.org

The Malaria Consortium is an international organization dedicated to improving the prevention and treatment of malaria in Africa and Asia. The organization maintains most of its offices and programs in these two continents. The group's Web site offers an extensive collection of articles about malaria as well as many links to additional informational resources concerning the disease.

National Foundation for Infectious Diseases (NFID)
4733 Bethesda Ave., Ste. 750, Bethesda, MD   20814
(301) 656-0003
Web site: www.nfid.org

NFID is a nonprofit organization whose mission is to educate the public and health-care workers about the causes, treatment, and prevention of infectious diseases. The organization's Web site includes a media center, fact sheets, and publications as well as specific information on meningitis, pertussis, tetanus, diphtheria, influenza, pneumococcal bacteria, and shingles (herpes zoster).

The National Patient Safety Foundation
132 MASS MoCA Way, North Adams, MA   01247
(413) 663-8900
e-mail: info@npsf.org
Web site: www.npsf.org

The National Patient Safety Foundation is a nonprofit advocacy group dedicated to improving patient safety. The foundation's Web site includes significant information on MRSA infections and prevention as well as publications, articles, and links to other sources of information concerning hospital patients and infectious diseases.

The National Vaccine Information Center (NVIC)
407 Church St., Ste. H, Vienna, VA   22180
(703) 938-0342
Web site: www.nvic.org

The National Vaccine Information Center is a nonprofit educational organization. According to the NVIC Web site, the organization is "dedicated to the prevention of vaccine injuries and deaths through public education and to defending the informed consent ethic." NVIC also helps people who believe they or their family members have been injured by vaccines. The organization's Web site includes many informative articles, a blog, and links to other news sources providing information about vaccines.

The Office of the Public Health Service Historian
695 Parklawn Bldg., Rockville, MD   20857
(301) 443-5363
Web site: http://lhncbc.nlm.nih.gov/apdb/phsHistory/

The Office of the Public Health Service Historian is the gateway to the history of public health in the United States. The site contains extensive and accessible information about the 1918 influenza pandemic as well as multimedia exhibits, a section on health and the news, an extensive collection of photographs, and a large bibliography.

PandemicFlu.gov
U.S. Department of Health and Human Services
Washington, DC 20201
Web site: www.pandemicflu.gov

This Department of Health and Human Services site offers a large, up-to-date, resource that provides one-stop access to all U.S. government information regarding avian and pandemic influenza. It includes sections on health and safety, global issues, articles on the economic impact of flu, a newsroom, and a glossary. This site is essential for the student interested in bird flu and the likelihood of a future pandemic.

Vaccine and Infectious Disease Organization (VIDO)
University of Saskatchewan, Saskatoon, SK S7N 5E3
    Canada
(306) 966-7478
Web site: www.vido.org

The Vaccine and Infectious Disease Organization is a non-profit organization owned by the University of Saskatchewan and supported by the governments of Alberta and Saskatchewan as well as the Canadian government. Its work centers on the development and delivery of new vaccines for humans and animals. VIDO's Web site includes news about its work, publications, and information about careers and training in the field of immunology.

The Vaccine Education Center
The Children's Hospital of Philadelphia
Philadelphia, PA 19104
(215) 590-1000
Web site: www.chop.edu

The Vaccine Education Center of the Children's Hospital of Philadelphia provides complete and reliable information about vaccines. This information includes videos, DVDs, news articles, and publications. The site also includes a schedule of recommended vaccinations. Readers can order additional educational materials through its Web site. Links to other high-quality resources extend the helpfulness of the site.

World Health Organization (WHO)
Avenue Appia 20, Geneva 27   1211
  Switzerland
+41 22 791-21-11
e-mail: info@who.int
Web site: www.who.int

The World Health Organization is the United Nations' directing and coordinating authority for health. As such, WHO is a global force in issues of health and disease. The WHO Web site includes multimedia presentations, fact sheets, news articles, publications, brochures, and statistics. An essential starting place for any student of infectious disease, the Web site also offers online books for downloading and information on ordering materials through the mail.

Bibliography

Books

Arthur Allen	*Vaccine: The Controversial Story of Medicine's Greatest Lifesaver.* New York: Norton, 2007.
John Barry	*The Great Influenza: The Epic Story of the Deadliest Plague in History.* New York: Viking, 2004.
Debbie Bookchin	*The Virus and the Vaccine: The True Story of a Cancer-Causing Monkey Virus, Contaminated Polio Vaccine, and the Millions of Americans Exposed.* New York: St. Martin's, 2004.
Alfred W. Crosby	*America's Forgotten Pandemic: The Influenza of 1918.* 2nd ed. Cambridge: Cambridge University Press, 2003.
Pete Davies	*The Devil's Flu: The World's Deadliest Influenza Epidemic and the Scientific Hunt for the Virus That Caused It.* New York: Henry Holt, 2000.
John DiConsiglio	*When Birds Get Flu and Cows Go Mad! How Safe Are We?* New York: Franklin Watts, 2008.
Toyin Falola and Matthew M. Heaton	*HIV/AIDS, Illness, and African Well-Being.* Rochester, NY: University of Rochester Press, 2007.

I.W. Fong and
Ken Alibek

New and Evolving Infections of the 21st Century. New York: Springer, 2007.

Sean M. Grady
and John Tabak

Biohazards: Humanity's Battle with Infectious Disease. New York: Facts On File, 2006.

Norbert Gualde

Resistance: The Human Struggle Against Infection. Washington, DC: Dana Press, 2006.

Stuart A. Hill

Emerging Infectious Diseases. San Francisco: Pearson/Benjamin Cummings, 2006.

John Kelly

The Great Mortality: An Intimate History of the Black Death, the Most Devastating Plague of All Time. New York: HarperCollins, 2005.

Ann Marie
Kimball

Risky Trade: Infectious Disease in the Era of Global Trade. Burlington, VT: Ashgate, 2006.

Gina Kolata

Flu: The Story of the Great Influenza Pandemic of 1918 and the Search for the Virus That Caused It. New York: Farrar, Straus & Giroux, 1999.

Katherine E.
Korhn et al.

The 1918 Flu Pandemic. Mankato, MN: Capstone, 2008.

Felissa R. Lashley
and Jerry D.
Durham

Emerging Infectious Diseases: Trends and Issues. New York: Springer, 2007.

Kurt Link   *Understanding New, Resurgent, and
                         Resistant Diseases: How Man and
                         Globalization Create and Spread
                         Illness.* Westport, CT: Praeger, 2007.

Sharon Moalem   *Survival of the Sickest: A Medical
and Jonathan   Maverick Discovers Why We Need
Prince   Disease.* Westport, CT: Praeger, 2007.

Pete Moore   *The Little Book of Pandemics: 50 of
                         the World's Most Virulent Plagues and
                         Infectious Diseases.* New York:
                         HarperCollins, 2007.

A. Lloyd Moote   *The Great Plague: The Story of
and Dorothy C.   London's Most Deadly Year.* Baltimore:
Moote   Johns Hopkins University Press,
                         2004.

Randall M.   *The Making of a Tropical Disease: A
Packard   Short History of Malaria.* Baltimore:
                         Johns Hopkins University Press,
                         2007.

Jessica Snyder   *Good Germs, Bad Germs: Health and
Sachs   Survival in a Bacterial World.* New
                         York: Hill and Wang, 2008.

Teri Shors   *Understanding Viruses.* Boston: Jones
                         and Bartlett, 2008.

David Talan,   *Infectious Disease Emergencies.*
Gregory J. Moran,   Philadelphia: Elsevier Science, 2008.
and Frederick M.
Abrahamian

Priscilla Wald   *Contagious: Cultures, Carriers, and
                         the Outbreak Narrative.* Durham, NC:
                         Duke University Press, 2008.

Allen B. Weisse   *Lessons in Mortality: Doctors and Patients Struggling Together.* Columbia: University of Missouri Press, 2006.

Barbara Wexler   *Health and Wellness: Illness Among Americans.* Detroit: Thomson Gale, 2007.

Viroj Wiwanitkit   *Bird Flu: The New Emerging Infectious Disease.* New York: Nova Science, 2008.

Periodicals

Tim Appenzeller   "Tracking the Next Killer Flu," *National Geographic,* October 2005.

Jim Atkinson   "Hot Shot," *Texas Monthly,* April 2007.

Monya Baker   "Battling Evolution to Fight Antibiotic Resistance: Fresh Approaches Could Aid Existing Drugs," *Scientist,* October 10, 2005.

Betsy Bates   "Quicker, Simpler Tests Sought for MRSA Screening," *Skin & Allergy News,* February 2007.

S. Broor   "Recent Avian Influenza Outbreaks: A Pandemic in the Waiting," *Indian Journal of Medical Microbiology,* April/June 2005.

Hoosen Coovadia and Chifumbe Chintu "Pediatric Research: Filling the Gaps: As Horrible as the AIDS Epidemic Is, Easily Preventable Diseases Are Destroying the Children of Sub-Saharan Africa, Too," *Applied Clinical Trials*, January 2005.

Rocky Cranenburgh "Needle-Free Methods of Vaccination: Alternative Transdermal and Oral Vaccination Methods Are Being Developed to Improve Vaccine Delivery," *Biopharm International*, January 2008.

Jerome Groopman "Superbugs," *New Yorker*, August 11 and 18, 2008.

Godwin Haruna "What to Do with Malaria Challenge," *This Day*, April 29, 2008.

Paul Hunt "Poverty, Malaria and the Right to Health: Exploring the Connections," *UN Chronicle*, November 4, 2007.

Mary Anne Jackson "What Will Rate in '08 as Top Concerns? (Infectious Disease Consult)," *Pediatric News*, January 2008.

Robert Langreth "Booster Shot," *Forbes Global*, November 12, 2007.

George Luber and Jeremy Hess "Climate Change and Human Health in the United States," *Journal of Environmental Health*, December 2007.

Tony Mauro "The Future of Vaccines," *Miami Daily Business Review*, June 7, 2007.

David M. Morens and Anthony S. Fauci "The 1918 Influenza Pandemic: Insights for the 21st Century," *Journal of Infectious Diseases*, April 1, 2007.

David M. Morens, Jeffrey K. Taubenberger, and Anthony S. Fauci "Predominant Role of Bacterial Pneumonia as a Cause of Death in Pandemic Influenza: Implications for Pandemic Influenza Preparedness," *Journal of Infectious Diseases*, October 1, 2008.

Janice Nicholson "Infectious Disease Risk Increases as a Result of Climate Change," *CNW Group*, March 10, 2008.

NIH News "Bacterial Pneumonia Caused Most Deaths in 1918 Influenza Pandemic," August 19, 2008.

Janet Pelley "Will Climate Change Worsen Infectious Disease?" *Science News*, March 15, 2005.

Michael E. Pichichero "Feds Need Help to Bring Vaccines to U.S. Market," *Skin & Allergy News*, March 2008.

Michael E. Pichichero "No Vaccine-Autism Link in Feds' Ruling," *Pediatric News*, April 2008.

Peter Piot "Combating AIDS: What More Needs to Be Done?" *UN Chronicle*, November 4, 2007.

Nola M. Ries "Public Health Law and Ethics: Lessons from SARS and Quarantine," *LawNow*, February/March 2005.

Sydney Rosen et al.

"Hard Choices: Rationing Antiretroviral Therapy for HIV/AIDS in Africa," *Lancet*, January 22, 2005.

Jessica Snyder Sachs

"Target Better Health: If You Can't Remember the Last Time You Got a Vaccine, Call Your Doctor Now," *Prevention*, October 2007.

Ola Sheyin

"A New Approach to a Continuing Problem," *New African*, February 2005.

Dan Sorenson

"Measles Outbreak Not Subdued: Don't Take Immunity for Granted," *Arizona Daily Star*, May 2008.

Space Daily

"International Health Experts to Enlist the Public in War on African Malaria," April 24, 2008.

Miriam E. Tucker

"MMRV Vaccine Tied to Risk for Febrile Seizures," *Family Practice News*, March 15, 2008.

Breanne Wagner

"Germ Warfare: Agencies Scramble to Create Vaccine Market," *National Defense*, June 2007.

Jeffrey Young

"Five Years Later, Smallpox Preparedness Improved," *Hill*, May 13, 2008.

Index

A

A.J. Gallagher Risk Management Services, 36
Abraham, Janice, 35, 38, 40
ADHD (attention-deficit hyperactivity disorder), 73
Africa, 49, 51
Airport preparedness
  example situation, 57–60
  health officials' roles, 60–61
  precautions, 61–62
America's Forgotten Pandemic (Crosby), 7
Anopheles gambiae, 16
Anthrax, 19–20
Antibiotics
  discovery of, 10
  expense of resistance, 89–90
  renewed search for, 88
  resistance, 86–87
  use as prescribed, 87–88
Antimicrobial-resistant microorganisms, 13
Antiretroviral medications, 15
Appenzeller, Tim, 9
ArboNet, 112, 122
Arctic warming, 109
  See also Climate change
Arthritis, 73
Association for Professionals in Infection Control and Epidemiology (APIC), 92
Asthma, 72
Autism, 72
Avian flu, 10, 13, 17–18, 33, 44
  See also College campus risks

B

Baldvins, Lynn, 89–90
Barkin, Anita, 37–38
Barry, John, 7, 8
Bioterrorism, 19–20
Blueprint for Pandemic Flu Preparedness Planning for Colleges and Universities, 36
Bova, Alan, 34–35, 39
The British Medical Journal, 76
British National Childhood Encephalopathy Study, 77
Burkholderia pseudomallei, 107
Bush, George W., 29

C

Campylobacter, 107
Caribbean, 49, 52
Carnegie Mellon, 37–38
Censorship, 9
Center for Science in the Public Interest, 89
Centers for Disease Control and Prevention (CDC)
  adult immunization, 81–82
  antibiotic resistance, 86
  chronic disease/disability data, 72–73
  climate change preparation, 110–115
  Health Protection Goals, 115
  MRSA infections, 92
  pandemic preparation, 36
Chicken pox, 66–67
Chikungunya fever, 105